A CALL
for
CHARACTER

A CALL
for
CHARACTER

manifestation of the sons of God

GREG ZOSCHAK

TATE PUBLISHING *& Enterprises*

Published by Tate Publishing & Enterprises, LLC
127 E. Trade Center Terrace | Mustang, Oklahoma 73064 USA
1.888.361.9473 | www.tatepublishing.com

Tate Publishing is committed to excellence in the publishing industry. The company reflects the philosophy established by the founders, based on Psalms 68:11,
"The Lord gave the word and great was the company of those who published it."

Published in the United States of America

ISBN: 978-1-602474-1-6
04.04.17

DEDICATION

This book has been written now for several years and has recently been republished, to which my wife and I are truly grateful. This new printing has brought an opportunity to reflect back on the previous years and rewrite a dedication for A *Call for Character*. As young believers, we are set on a course to seek and know our Lord, who first loved us. In this pursuit, Jesus said "We all go through the rain, wind, and floods of life." It's in those seasons that life, family, and our future seem dark and dismal, but the Father has placed inside of us a seed of who He is, "The Greater One." The very expression of His character is the overcoming dynamic in life's struggles. When life says give up, your heart cries stand up. I dedicate this book to those who have heard the call of character over our storms of life. First and foremost to our four daughters who have stood together with us on the foundation of God's unfailing love. "Children's children are the crown of old men" (Proverbs 17:6). The greatest crown this side of heaven will be to see our four daughters raise their children in the nurture and admonition of the Lord. They have experienced His saving grace and now have crowned our life with grandchildren who will know *A Call to Character*.

CONTENTS

FOREWORD

I enthusiastically recommend Greg Zoschak's book entitled, *A Call for Character*. I think it is an excellent study of the fruit of the Spirit. One of our most important challenges today is for you and I to walk in the fruit of the Spirit and for that fruit to flow out of us.

Greg's book increases our understanding of the fruit of the Spirit and how it can be developed in our life. He also shows us that love, joy, peace, patience, goodness, kindness, faithfulness, gentleness, and self-control are powerful forces that are born into us when we are born of God. This fruit makes up our new nature and come from the nature of our heavenly Father. They will produce great victory in our life.

They are in you and can abound.

We are predestined to be conformed to the image of His Son—the Lord Jesus Christ. The fruit of the Spirit is born into us at conversion to cause a wonderful transformation from the inside out. It is so important that we learn to yield to this process. This book will help you do just that.

-Gloria Copeland

PREFACE

It is my prayer that through reading this book, believers will become aware of yet another benefit of the precious gift of the Holy Spirit and will allow God's Spirit to develop fruit in their lives.

Christians who follow the biblical principals as set forth by the teachings in this book, will be recognized as those professing Christians whose lives truly emanate the Christ-like qualities of love, joy, peace, longsuffering, gentleness, goodness, faith meekness, and temperance (Galatians 5:22, 23). All disputing over the controversial doctrine of the Holy Spirit must stop here, for against such character qualities, who can argue?

I encourage every Christian who, with a good and honest heart, desires the manifestation of the fruits in his life to read this book with an open heart and mind and be willing to receive all that the Holy Spirit has to offer—especially the character of Jesus.

-Greg Zoschak

INTRODUCTION

"For the earnest expectation of the creature waiteth for the manifestation of the sons of God."

Romans 8:19

What experienced believer would deny that his daily walk with God contained two seemingly passive elements—waiting and expecting? Whether spoken or unspoken, an expectation of that *manifestation of the Sons of God* rests within the mind of every professed Christian.

According to Romans 8:19, there will be a day when the sons of God will ultimately become manifest. All professed Christians expect to be included in this disclosure, but unfortunately most passively await its arrival. The concern of those who await and expect manifestation should obviously be: who exactly will be made manifest.

Romans 8:19 declares that it is the sons of God who will receive manifestation. In Greek, this particular word for sons is *huios* (hwee-os'), a word which emphasized the relationship of an offspring to its parent, especially the expression of the *character* or *nature* of that parent. Here, the Apostle Paul uses it to refer to the relationship of the children born into the family of God to their heavenly Father. The implication is that such children will be recognizable by their God-like qualities.

> *But as many as received him, to them gave he the power to become the sons of God, even to them that believe on his name: Which were born, not of blood, nor of the will of the flesh, nor of the will of man, but of God.*
>
> *John 1:12, 13*

The Greek word for sons in John 1:12 is not *huios* but *teknon (tek'non)*. Teknon emphasized the fact of birth rather than the dignity and character of the relationship between the offspring and the parent. According to Romans 8:19, it will be the *huios* who will be manifested, not the *teknon*. In other words, it is not those who have simply been born again who will be recognized as sons of God, but those who demonstrate the very nature and character of their heavenly Father.

Unfortunately, many people who are born again and baptized in the Holy Spirit have never developed an intimate personal relationship with their Father, and have never served Him collectively with their brothers and sisters in the Lord whether through church attendance, teaching a Sunday school class, tithing, or even performing good works. Outwardly, they may be acknowledged as "good Christians." The question is: are they recognized as the sons of God? If not, their "religion" is in vain because it does not reveal God's nature to the world.

Then, there are those who are willing to pay the price involved in developing a personal relationship with the Father. Although God is pleased when a believer serves Him collectively with others of like precious faith, His ultimate goal and desire for all of His children is that they come to know Him individually and develop an intimate relationship with Him. God wants His sons to get to know Him personally so they will take on His nature and character because these are what bring manifestation.

> *Isn't there within the hearts of every earthly father a sense of pride in seeing his child grow and become like him in personality, attitude and behavior? The same is true of the heavenly Father. God takes great fatherly pride in His sons, and He desires that they be readily identified as His.*

Romans 8:14 expounds on an identifiable trait of the sons of God: "For as many as are led by the Spirit of God, they are the sons of God." Again, the Greek word for sons is *huios*. Thus, one indication that Christians are indeed the sons of God is the fact that they are led by the Spirit of God. Most believers, however, do not have a clear understanding of exactly what this involves. When most church members think of being led by the Spirit, they usually picture in their minds a particular

Christian brother or sister who is reputed for often making reference to the fact that God told them to do this or that, and they felt compelled to obey.

Even though having this ability to hear the voice of God and then act on it is a part of what it means to be led by the Spirit, it is by no means all that is involved. Being led of God's Spirit (His nature) implies not only being obedient to the voice of the Spirit but also developing the character of God.

Some believers are in obedience to the voice of God in that they willingly obey His will as it is revealed to them, yet they obey Him in the wrong spirit. For example, some are being led by the Spirit to a degree, but many times they become arrogant in their actions or attitudes. They reason that whenever God speaks to their hearts, they are being called upon to carry out His will whatever the cost. They then justify their rude actions and arrogant attitude by saying, "But God told me to do it." Thus, they carry out God's will in the wrong spirit, even though the right Spirit prompted them.

Being led by the Spirit, therefore, is twofold. First, it is receiving instruction from God. Second, it is fulfilling the will of God in the spirit (character) of Jesus.

In Romans 8:29, the Apostle Paul plainly states that God desires that the individual characters of His children undergo a transformational process and become identical with the character of Jesus: "For whom he did foreknow, he also did predestinate to be conformed to the image of his Son, that he might be the firstborn among many brethren." The heavenly Father wills that

His numerous *adopted* sons be conformed to the image of His only *begotten* Son, Jesus. This conformation is necessary in order for the family of God to live in unity and thus fulfill the Father's will concerning how a family should function in their relationships.

Being conformed to the image of Jesus simply means taking on His form, His likeness, His stature or resemblance. When all of God's children are conformed to the character and the likeness of His only begotten Son, Jesus, then and only then will it become evident that they are led by the Spirit and truly are the sons of God. The whole of creation awaits this glorious day of revelation!

Developing the character of Jesus is accomplished by developing the same fruit that were easily recognized in His life. Jesus Himself taught in Matthew 7 that it is by outward manifestation (fruit) that inward nature (character) is recognized:

> *Beware of false prophets, which come to you in sheep's clothing, but inwardly they are ravening wolves. Ye shall know them by their fruits. Do men gather grapes of thorns, or figs of thistles? ... Wherefore by their fruits ye shall know them.*
>
> *vv. 15, 16, 20*

When Jesus said, "ye shall know them," He was speaking to His disciples about false prophets. But doesn't the world also watch the lives of professed Christians?

The world must be able to recognize the true sons of God. They recognize them by their fruits!

Contrary to the thinking of today in many churches on this issue, Jesus did not say, "Ye shall know them by *their miracles.*" Neither did He say, "Ye shall know them by the *number of verses they can quote.*" He did not even say, "Ye shall know them by *how loudly they speak in tongues.*" Jesus said, "Ye shall know them by *their fruits.*" In essence, He said, "You shall recognize My disciples by their *character.*"

The character-building fruits Jesus is speaking of are listed in Galatians 5:22, 23:

> But the fruit of the Spirit is love, joy, peace, longsuffering, gentleness, goodness, faith, Meekness, temperance: against such there is no law.

Accordingly, these are the *fruits,* not the *gifts,* of the Spirit. There is a difference between the fruits of the Spirit and the gifts of the Spirit, which are listed in Romans 12:6–8 and 1 Corinthians 12:8–10. These gifts—a few of which are wisdom, knowledge, prophecy, tongues, and the working of miracles—are merely given by God to believers, bestowed upon them by His grace.

The means of acquiring the fruits of the Spirit, however, are quite different. Fruit must be cultivated, and that requires time and effort. A cost is definitely involved in the development of the fruits of the Spirit. This is the reason why many believers operate in the gifts, but don't give evidence of any fruit. Although, when we become born again the seed of the fruit of the Spirit is imparted to us as a believer and His character is planted inside of us. The maturity of the seed is our responsibility. People are simply not willing to pay the price to produce fruit. This is also the reason why many believers who serve and function in the gifts and even operate in them under a tremendous anointing, are some of the rudest people imaginable. Believers who operate in the gifts may even perform many miraculous signs and wonders, but they can still be uncouth and unlikable.

Operating in the gifts of the Spirit does not ensure that a person will possess the character of Jesus!

Because of the easy accessibility of the gifts, there is a real danger in the charismatic movement of emphasizing the gifts at the expense of the fruits! This is dangerous because the main purpose of the gifts is to produce the fruits. Perhaps the reason believers prefer to substitute the gifts and good works for the fruits of God's Spirit is because the fruits must be cultivated through time and effort. Jesus said in Mark 4:28, 29:

For the earth bringeth forth fruit of herself; first the blade, then the ear, after that the full corn in the ear. But when the fruit is brought forth, immediately he putteth in the sickle, because the harvest is come.

The fact that the development of fruit is a growth process is even taught in the laws of nature—the mightiest of fruit-bearing trees begins as a mere blade. The same is true in the spiritual realm. Every believer is a "fruit tree." The stage of development of the fruits differs with each individual.

For example, one person may have been cultivating the fruit of temperance in his life, and that fruit may be largely developed; whereas in another person the fruit of temperance is not quite as well developed, because he had been cultivating the fruit of kindness.

It is those people who have developed all their fruit who will be most manifest. Believers cannot become selective so that they cultivate only those fruits that offer the least resistance to their personality type or their flesh. For example, a believer who is an extrovert cannot say, because of his assertive personality, "I choose to develop the fruit of faith, but not the fruit of longsuffering." Believers must develop all of the fruits, for none of them are optional.

Jesus Christ is coming back to the earth for people who have been conformed to His image—for those who must be striving to develop one hundredfold of all the fruits, for Jesus Himself was one hundredfold. It is absurd to think that our Lord was selective of the fruits He bore. Who can imagine Jesus bearing thirty fold of patience or sixty fold of love? Instead, His life bore a hundredfold of all nine fruits.

In order for us to greatly desire the fruits of the Spirit in our lives, it is vital for us to fully understand the function of each fruit. For those people who have the fruits developed in their lives in varying degrees, understanding their functions will bring a greater appreciation of those fruits and perhaps instill a greater hunger for still more cultivation. Spiritual development and production should never stop.

Each fruit of the Spirit enables the individual believer to better cope with adverse situations that arise in his life. There is not any situation, trial, or temptation that a child of God will face that one of the fruits of the Spirit will not enable him to overcome. Because of His love, the Father yearns for His children to begin to cultivate every fruit of the Spirit, for He wants His sons to be overcomers. Actually, a believer cannot be a totally successful overcomer if any one of the fruits is missing in his life, because that particular area will be the very one in which the devil will concentrate his attack.

It is also vital for us, as believers, to become knowledgeable about how to cultivate each fruit individually and then begin developing the fruits in our lives. Though it does require time and effort, the rewards gained will far surpass the cost involved.

Also, though developing the fruits may seem like an impossible task, the Father would not expect the impossible of His children. He does require diligent cultivation through obedience to His Word, but beyond that, no amount of fear or worry will produce any desired spiritual result. Anxious thoughts such as, "How could I possibly mature and develop fruits like Jesus?" may discourage some from even trying to develop their maturity and prevent them from ever beginning to cultivate the fruits in their lives.

When thinking in terms of spiritual growth, we must realize the truth of 1 Corinthians 3:5, 6 that it is always God who gives the increase. In Matthew 6:24–34, Jesus soothed the minds of His disciples concerning the Father's faithfulness in providing for their material needs. After proper cultivation has begun in their lives, God's children today can take comfort in a spiritual sense from verse 28: "Consider the lilies of the field, how they grow."

The Word of God clearly explains how to develop each fruit of the Spirit. The sooner we believers choose to begin the process of cultivating, the sooner that blade, that ear, and that full corn will appear in our individual lives.

THE GREATEST
COMMANDMENT

"But the fruit of the Spirit is love..."
Galatians 5:22

When most believers think of the fruit of love, they usually think automatically in terms of cultivating and developing love relationships toward their brothers and sisters in Christ. Although this is necessary, in that God commands it of His children, it is not all that is involved in love. There is yet another, more important aspect of the fruit of love. *To truly be perfect even as his Father in heaven is perfect, each child of God must diligently cultivate and develop an individual love relationship with his heavenly Father.*

Many Christians today do not seem to realize that the Great Commandment is not, "Love one another." According to Jesus in Matthew 22:37–39, a believer can love the brethren in proper perspective only after first loving God:

Jesus said unto him, Thou shalt love the Lord thy God

with all thy heart, and with all thy soul, and with all thy mind. This is the first and great commandment. And the second is like unto it, Thou shalt love thy neighbor as thyself.

Actually, some Christians express more love to others in the Body of Christ than they express to God. The reason they do this is simply because they are just not comfortable in expressing the love in their hearts directly to the Father. There really is no reasonable explanation for some of God's beloved children finding it easier to express more love to one another than to their Father Who loves them to the extent that He gave His only begotten Son to die on their behalf (John 3:16). Unfortunately, however, this is the case with many in the family of God today.

Most believers would feel quite comfortable in sitting down, conversing with, and somehow expressing love to other members of the Body of Christ. How would they act, however, if Jesus Christ, in the flesh, were to walk into the room for the purpose of sitting down with them and conversing with them personally? Would they be as relaxed and comfortable expressing love to Him as they would to another Christian? Aside from the sensationalism that the thought of such a miraculous happening would cause, in all honesty, would not most believers be ill at ease in such a one-on-one encounter with Jesus? Why? Is it, perhaps, because to them He is merely an acquaintance and not a close, intimate friend?

In biblical times, many called God "Father," but few personally ministered love to Jesus (Who was, after all,

Emmanuel—God with us) through such acts as washing and kissing His feet (Luke 7:38) or anointing His head (Mark 14:3) or taking the time to return and say, "Thank You" (Luke 17:15, 16). God desires that His children know Him to the extent that they are as comfortable in expressing love to Him as they are in their closest, most intimate relationship on earth. Only then, will the children of God come to know the Father in the Spirit as well as they know the people dearest to them in the flesh.

Knowing the Father to this extent on earth will be the source of our confidence when we each stand before the Son of God on that day that is yet to come (John 14:8, 9). Many people today totally rely on expressing their love to the Father indirectly through doing good works. In that day when they stand before Him, they will be rejected by Him.

Jesus said in Matthew 7:22 "Many will say to me in that day, Lord, Lord, have we not prophesied in thy name? And in they name have cast out devils? And in thy name done many wonderful works?" According to Jesus, one basis of His rejection of such people in that day will be expressed in the words, "I never knew you"(v. 23). This Greek word for knew is *ginosko (ghin-oce'-ko)* which means "to know by experience or effort; knowledge as the result of prolonged practice; knowledge grounded in personal experience; to get to know." In essence, Jesus will be saying: "I never got to know you, for you did not cultivate that fruit of love and develop an intimate, loving relationship with Me." Therefore, it will greatly benefit us believers in that day if we will begin to develop a love relationship with the Father by cultivating this powerful fruit of love today.

In addition to future blessings, there are two present benefits for those who develop the fruit of love toward the Father. The first of these two benefits is found in 1 John 4:18 "There is no fear in love; but perfect love casteth out fear: because fear hath torment. He that feareth is not made perfect in love."

There is a part that cultivating the presence of love for the Father plays concerning walking in total absence of fear. Of course, there is also an important part that binding, rebuking, and casting out the spirit of fear plays in walking in peace. But when believers faithfully cast out the spirit without permanent relief from fear, perhaps they should seriously consider whether they really need to simply cultivate love for the Father.

People can cast out the spirit of fear in their lives until they are "blue in the face," but if their lives are devoid of that perfect love for the Father, then their houses will be empty of the one quality that will prevent this particular spirit from returning to take up residence.

"He that feareth is not made perfect in love." Wanting the best for His children, the Father is pleading for them to realize the benefits of developing a close personal relationship with Him. He is encouraging us to begin cultivating that perfect love by offering us total absence of fear. It will be a growth process, but the more we believers increase our love for the Father, the more fear will decrease in our lives. Is not the Father's offer of total absence of fear sufficient incentive for us as His children to begin the process of the cultivation of love?

The Father knew of the abundant, increasing danger of this cancerous fear in today's society. In Luke 21:26 Jesus Himself forewarned of the fear which was yet to come in our day: "Men's hearts failing them for fear, and for looking after those things which are coming on the earth: for the powers of heaven shall be shaken." It is more than an added benefit of living without fear that we cultivate the fruit of love with the Father; in today's society especially, it is vital to our very health and well-being.

Many people today are dying of heart attacks in fulfillment of Jesus' prophecy that heart failure would be one of the indications and direct consequences of fear. The world is fast approaching a time when fear of Satan and fear of circumstances will grip the hearts of men and women to a greater degree than ever before. Fear of the unstable economic system and fear of the world system in general can already be seen gripping the hearts of men and women around the globe. Yet, the world today is experiencing only the beginning of birth pains as the "...*whole creation groaneth and travaileth in pain together until now*" (Romans 8:22).

If ever there was a time when there was a need to develop a love relationship with the Father, it is right now, because this fear is even slipping to the hearts of believers and gripping them in its deadly vice. Believers who are vulnerable to fear and whose hearts are its easy prey are those who, even though they have been "delivered...from the power of darkness" (Colossians 1:13) still have their minds and affections set on things contained therein. Therefore, all of us should be cultivating with God so that as fear increases about us in our society, so will our love increase within us for our Father and thus offset the fear.

It is imperative that we believers combat fear with love because fear will lead to many negative things in our lives. Fear is the root of many of the problems that have manifested themselves in individuals in the Church today. Generally speaking, fear leads to sickness, oppression, and even death. Truly, it is an ugly spirit that is capable of even stopping a person's heart from beating once it has taken root in it. For this reason, Jesus especially warned the people of His day to be aware of this increasingly dangerous spirit and to take precautions against it by developing their individual relationships with the Father, before the powers of heaven are really shaken.

Jesus not only warned His followers of the fear to come, He also presented them with an image of the Father that would encourage them to cultivate His perfect love:

> *Are not two sparrows sold for a farthing? And one of them shall not fall on the ground without your Father. But the very hairs of your head are all numbered. Fear ye not therefore, ye are of more value than many sparrows. (Matthew 10:29–31).*

Jesus said, "Fear ye not therefore..." The word therefore

in verse 31 is an implied reference to the two previous scriptures. Jesus was telling His followers: "When a sparrow drops to the ground, the Father knows about it. The very hairs of your head are numbered; therefore, fear not." What He was telling His disciples was that if they would develop a relationship with God to the point of fully realizing their loving Father's infinite awareness of them, they would no longer fear. A believer does not come to this abiding and sustaining knowledge at the precise moment of being born again; this kind of awareness only comes through cultivation.

Most believers, however, are not cultivating that love or coming to that awareness. This is the reason there is so much fear in their lives. Today, when most Christians hear the shrill scream of a tornado siren, fear immediately grips their hearts as they anxiously watch the dark storm clouds mount in the sky. Once given evidence, that fear attempts to take root. If allowed to do so, it will eventually manifest its presence through mental oppression, physical or emotional illness, or even death. At the first sound of the siren or at the first whisper of an approaching storm, however, we believers should remember that Jesus is still saying to us, "Fear ye not therefore..."

When the lump of growth appears, many believers are immediately gripped with fear as they envision their "helpless" bodies being invaded by that dreaded disease, cancer. But God's Word does not change. Jesus is still saying, "Fear ye not therefore..." The cancer of fear is a greater enemy to many Christians than the physical disease itself. Fear can be deadly if not handled properly, according to the Word of God.

When many people hear of tragic events through the media, news of some impending danger that threatens to invade their world and upset the peace and tranquility of their lives, fear immediately grips their hearts. But regardless of the increasing state of chaotic madness of this enormous mental institution called the world, Jesus is still saying, "Fear ye not therefore..."

So why do believers fear? They fear because they do not know that their loving, omniscient Father has the very hairs on their heads numbered. According to Acts 10:38, Jesus healed all who were oppressed of the devil. God desires to heal His children today of the oppression of fear though His perfect love. The Father wants His children to cultivate a relationship with Him to the point that they understand Him and know that He understands them. He wants them to comprehend Him as their omniscient Father whose wisdom and knowledge are infinite. He desires that they realize He has known His children from the foundation of the world and has ordained every single step they take in life.

This kind of relationship, however, must be cultivated and developed. The more we believers develop that awareness of God's love and faithfulness, the less we fear. Hebrews 13:5, 6 declares:

...he hath said, I will never leave thee, nor forsake thee. So that we may boldly say, The Lord is my helper, and I will not fear what man shall do unto me.

The Father wants His children to see Him as their Helper. The Greek word for helper in this passage is quite unique, for it is a compound word that means to run to one's aid. The Father does not want His children to picture Him in their minds as procrastinating when they are in trouble, because in reality He runs to their aid. When we Christians begin to see God as our divine "Helper," and as we begin to understand the full measure of that term, then we will begin to boldly say: "We will not fear what man does, what the world does, or what the enemy does, because the Lord is our Helper."

According to Hebrews 11:27, it was for this reason that Moses did not fear Pharaoh when he left Egypt. "By faith he forsook Egypt, not fearing the wrath of the king: for he endured, as seeing him who is invisible." The more we believers develop our own individual love relationship with our Father, the clearer we will see Him, and the less we will fear.

The second benefit of developing the fruit of love toward the Father is that it enables a person to conquer all things. According to 1 Corinthians 13:8, "love never fails." Since God is love (1 John 4:8), this must mean that He can never fail. Therefore, the more we develop our love for Him, then the less we will fail in our individual lives, for we will know Him as Conqueror. Like Paul, we will then develop the attitude: "What shall we say then to these things? If God be for us, who can be against us?" (Romans 8:31).

As believers cultivate and develop love for the Father,

an awareness of Him as Conqueror will increase, and confidence in His willingness and His ability to make *them* conquerors will become manifest in their lives. "God is for me" is quite a confident statement.

But there are many Christians today who cannot proclaim it honestly from their hearts. When they encounter trials and temptations, they feel that they are all alone. The reason for this feeling is simply that they have not developed an individual love relationship with the Father. However, when a believer does take the initiative and does develop that relationship, then like Paul he will confidently ask: "Since God is for me, who can be against me?" The answer, of course, is no one, for God is Conqueror of all.

Desiring to conquer the works of the enemy in their lives, many Christians quote the familiar promise contained in Romans 8:28 without fully realizing the condition attached to it: "And we know that all things work together for good to them that love God, to them who are the called according to his purpose." All things work together for the good of whom? The answer is clearly stated: "...them that love God." The more believers love God, the more they will conquer trials and the more things will work together for their good. It is possible to go through trials and for the good received from the trials to be limited, but as a person's love for God grows and matures, he will discover that his trials are working good for him to a greater and greater degree.

In the midst of our trials, it is possible for us believers to measure the extent of our love relationship with

God. If we find ourselves fearfully running from the arms of the Lord instead of cleaving to Him, it is probable that a need exists in our lives to cultivate a greater love relationship with our heavenly Father. Since good comes from being in His presence, then loving God to the extent of cleaving to Him, even during the trials of life, will result in those trials working together for our good.

Thus, there is an inseparable relationship between the degree to which a believer conquers all things and the degree of development of his relationship with God. The single most important thing for us to be doing today is cultivating and developing a love relationship with our heavenly Father. Without that, anything else we attempt to do will be futile—it will be a work of the flesh; it will be hard, frustrating, and condemning. It is only when we come to a clear comprehension that God is for us personally, that God is our Helper, and that we are more than conquerors only through Him, that we are really going to overcome.

Believers must be taught how to take the little seed of love in their spirits and cultivate it into a healthy plant raising its head towards the heavenly Father. Every child of God should have this testimony: "I love God more than I did a year ago; therefore, I don't fear like I used to. Because of this, I now overcome something that used to defeat me." In essence, believers who cultivate their love for the Father may boldly say with Paul: "Nay, in all these things we are more than conquerors through him that loved us" (Romans 8:37).

Getting to know the heavenly Father is the key to victorious Christian living!

This is the one thing that religion is missing. Religion has the form of godliness, but it has left out God. Charismatics are not exempt from this danger, for they, too, can have the form of being religious but still forget the Lord. Even though a person may have been born again and filled with the Spirit, it is possible for him to go to charismatic churches until Jesus comes again and yet not even know God. Developing a love relationship with the Father involves more than having an experience. Just as a person can get married and never rally get to know his spouse, a believer can be born again and baptized in the Holy Spirit yet never get to know the heavenly Father. We need to realize that these spiritual experiences are for the purpose of bringing us into a cleaving relationship with the Father and begin to utilize them to this end.

We must also learn the specific steps involved in cultivating the fruit of love toward the Father until it grows and develops and matures so that we become like Enoch, walking with God day and night: "And Enoch walked with God: and he was not; for God took him" (Genesis 5:24). Believers with this hope must have this testimony—that they pleased God. (Hebrews 11:5). According to Hebrews 11:6, no one can please God without having faith. Many people do not fully understand the close relationship between having faith in God and knowing Him through the development of the fruit of love.

There are charismatic believers today who are going through a religious routine, but are not doing the one thing God called His Church to do—have faith in Him, which requires trust. According to Psalm 9:10, a person must know God before he can trust Him: "And they that know thy name will put their trust in thee: for thou, Lord, hast not forsaken them that seek thee." Therefore, to have faith in God actually means to know God.

There are believers today who are hearing teaching on faith, but who do not even know the Lord. Yet, they are being expected to trust God to move the mountains in their lives. The result of this is that they are experiencing failure, frustration and condemnation.

In Mark 11:22, Jesus first said, "Have faith in God," before He taught in verse 23 on speaking to the mountain and in verse 24 on praying and receiving. Believers, today, should be taught verse 22 *before* they are taught verse 23 and 24. In order to thoroughly develop faith in God, we need first to come to know God. We do that by learning to cultivate the fruit of love towards Him. To know Him is to love Him. To love Him is to trust Him. To trust Him is to have faith in Him—faith which moves mountains. It is then, and only then, that the heart receives its desires.

There are three steps involved in cultivating the fruit of love toward the heavenly Father. The first step of the cultivation process is to develop sight of God. In other words, a believer needs to sharpen his vision of the Father and thereby become more enlightened as to His personal attributes:

Be ye therefore followers of God, as dear children; And walk in love as Christ also hath loved us, and hath given himself for us as an offering and a sacrifice to God for a sweet smelling savor.

Ephesians 5:1, 2

According to these scriptures, we are to be imitators of God and walk in love, just as Jesus walked in love toward us. To walk in love as Jesus did is surely the heart's desire of every true believer. What was Jesus' source of victory that enabled Him to walk in love? He possessed nothing that we believers today do not possess, but He did know how to develop love in His life so that it produced one-hundredfold fruit. Since God commands His children to imitate Jesus in His love-walk, then we must know how He cultivated and developed this particular fruit in His life. This way in which He did this is found in John 5:17–19:

But Jesus answered them, My Father worketh hitherto, and I work. Therefore, the Jews sought the more to kill him, because he not only had broken the Sabbath, but said also that God was his Father, making himself equal with God. Then answered Jesus and said unto them, Verily, verily, I say to you, The Son can do nothing of himself, but what he seeth the Father do: for what things soever he doeth, these also doeth the Son likewise.

The source of Jesus' victory that enabled Him to walk in

love is found in verse 19: "The son can do nothing himself, but what he seeth the Father do." We must follow this example of Jesus if we expect to walk in love as He did. Many believers, however, are trying to act like the Son without seeing the Father. Jesus said that the Son could do nothing in Himself, and the same is true of us today—we cannot walk in love without spending time with the Father.

How often believers with good intentions and honest desires become frustrated as they try to walk in love, simply because they are trying to act like the Son but are not developing their sight of the Father. It is only as we imitate the example of Jesus and spend time in the Word and in the Spirit developing our love for the Father that the fruit of love will become manifest in our lives and will enable us to walk in love as Jesus did.

First John 4:7 and 8 reiterates that it is only as we know God that we will know how to love one another:

Beloved, let us love one another: for love is of God; and every one that loveth is born of God, and knoweth God. He that loveth not knoweth not God; for God is love.

Knowing God requires spending time alone with Him. Matthew 14:1–4 is an account of the death of John the Baptist. Within it is a beautiful story of how Jesus spent time with the Father and thereby cultivated and developed the fruit of love in His life.

Matthew 14:3–11 explains that Herod placed John

in prison for Herodias' sake . After the daughter of Herodias danced before Herod and pleased the king, he swore that he would give her anything she asked. After consulting with her mother, she asked for and received the head of John the Baptist on a charger.

"And his disciples came, and took up the body, and buried it, and went and told Jesus" (Matthew 14:12). John's disciples went and told Jesus what had happened to John. At this time, John the Baptist was perhaps the only person who fully realized who Jesus really was and what His plan and purpose was in life—that He was the Lamb of God Who would take away the sin of the world. Suddenly, Jesus heard that because some woman had danced before Herod and pleased him, John lost his life.

Could it be that Jesus was tempted not to walk in love? In such a case as this, being angry and wanting to retaliate would be the expected response of the flesh. According to Hebrews 4:15, Jesus "...was in all points tempted like as we are, yet without sin." But what happened?

"When Jesus heard of it, he departed thence by ship into a desert place apart: and when the people had heard thereof, they followed him on foot out of the cities" (Matthew 14:13). Jesus overcame this particular tempta-tion by separating Himself, by spending time alone with the Father and developing His sight of Him. Although this incident could have threatened to distort His image of God, Jesus made the effort immediately to develop a clear picture of Him as the loving, omniscient Father Who knew the number of the hairs of His head.

If we believers today would respond as Jesus did to adverse situations that threaten to distort a clear image of the Father, then we would be spared bitterness and resentment toward Him. We would come to know Him, and thereby cultivate the fruit of love in our individual lives. This was exactly what happened in this situation in the life of Jesus.

"And Jesus went forth, and saw a great multitude, and was moved with compassion toward them, and he healed their sick" (v. 14). The result of Jesus' developing sight of the Father, following the death of John the Baptist was that when he came into contact with people, He was moved with compassion—not bitterness nor resentment—because the fruit of love had been cultivated and developed in His life through loving the Father.

The second step to developing the fruit of love is to pray in the Spirit:

> But ye, beloved, building up yourselves on your most holy faith, praying in the Holy Ghost. Keep yourselves in the love of God, looking for the mercy of our Lord Jesus Christ unto eternal life.
>
> Jude 20, 21

According to this passage, praying in the Holy Ghost keeps the love of God stirred up and thereby cultivates it.

The life of Peter is an example of how praying in the Spirit cultivates the fruit of love:

> *So when they had dined, Jesus saith to Simon Peter, Simon, son of Jonas, lovest thou me more than these? He saith unto him, Yea, Lord; thou knowest that I love thee. He saith unto him, Feed my lambs. He saith to him again the second time, Simon, son of Jonas, lovest thou me? He saith unto him, Yea, Lord; thou knowest that I love thee. He saith unto him, Feed my sheep. He saith unto him the third time, Simon, son of Jonas, lovest thou me? Peter was grieved because he said unto him the third time, Lovest thou me? And he said unto him, Lord, thou knowest all things; thou knowest that I love thee. Jesus saith unto him, Feed my sheep.*

An understanding of the different Greek words for love will make this portion of Scripture clearer by giving us a better understanding of what Jesus was trying to emphasize to Peter. In verse 15, Jesus literally asked Peter, "Simon, son of Jonas, *agape* thou me more than these?" *Agape (ag-ah-pay)* refers to the God-kind of love or unconditional love; it is the type of love that will continue to love people regardless of whether or not it receives a response.

In verse 15, Peter literally responded, "Yea, Lord thou knowest that I *phileo* thee." *Phileo (fil-eh'-o)* is the Greek word for love that is conditional; in other words, the kind of love that changes according to the response it receives.

The third time however, Jesus asked him in verse 17, "Simon, son of Jonas, *phileo* thou me?" Jesus dropped down from an unconditional love to a love that is conditional, and, "Peter was grieved because he said unto him the third time, *Phileo* thou me?" He was grieved because he recognized that Jesus had changed to an expression of conditional love. He admitted, to an expression of conditional love. He admitted, "Lord, thou knowest all things; thou knowest that I *phileo* thee." Peter was in need of cultivating his love relationship with his Lord.

At this point in his life, Peter has already been born again, for in John 20: 21, 22, he received the work of the Holy Spirit in regeneration:

> *Then Jesus said to them again, Peace be unto you: as my Father hath sent me, even so sent I you. And when he had said this, he breathed on them, and saith unto them, Receive ye the Holy Ghost.*

In 1 Peter 1:7–8, Peter expressed a relationship with Jesus that he could not express in John 21:15–17:

That the trial of your faith, being much more precious than of gold that perisheth, though it be tried with fire, might be found unto praise and honour and glory at the appearing of Jesus Christ: Whom having not seen, ye love...

In the Greek, Peter is literally writing in verse 8, "Whom having not seen, ye *agape*." Something took place in Peter's life between John 21: 15–17 and 1 Peter 1:7–8 that enabled him to express the *agape* type of love to Jesus, What occurred in his life is recorded in Acts 2:4—he was baptized in the Holy Spirit and spoke in tongues: "And they were all filled with the Holy Ghost, and began to speak with other tongues, as the Spirit gave them utterance."

One of the first things believers should notice following their receiving the baptism of the Holy Spirit is that their love for God greatly increases, because the purpose of this experience is to bring the children of God into a closer love walk with their Father. "For he that speaketh in an unknown tongue speaketh not unto men, but unto God: for no man understandeth him; howbeit in the spirit he speaketh mysteries" (1 Corinthians 14:2). We believers should therefore utilize this experience to cultivate our individual relationship with the Father, by coming into His presence and praying intimately unto Him from our spirit, for that is one of the purposes of tongues.

The third step in developing love is to practice love. John states that God's love is perfected in those believers who love one another:

"No man hat seed God at any time. If we love one another, God dwelleth in us, and his love is perfected in us" (1 John 4:12).

The main hindrance in showing love to one another is the tendency to wait for a feeling prior to taking some type of action that would somehow express love. But love is not a feeling. Since God is love (1 John 4:8) and God is the Word (John 1:1), then love is putting the Word of God into practice. If we do that, we will be cultivating the fruit of love in our lives. Too many times, however, we wait for some type of a feeling, and nothing is accomplished in our lives as far as the fruit of love is concerned.

For instance, there may be a believer who has unforgiveness toward someone who has wronged him. He may know that God's Word says to do in this situation: "Moreover if thy brother shall trespass against thee, go and tell him his fault between thee and him alone: if he shall hear thee, thou hast gained thy brother" (Matthew 18:15). This believer may pray and fast and do everything imaginable, except what the Word says to do. When asked why he is not practicing Matthew 18:15, he will likely respond: "I can't go to that person just yet because I don't feel like I have forgiven him." The feeling of love, however, would come through acting out Matthew 18:15, for that is how love is perfected—by being a doer of the Word and not just a hearer.

Remember: Feeling follows action.

The same principle is true of cultivating a relationship with the Father. There are many believers who want to cultivate their relationship with God, so they begin praying in the Spirit for a short time. Then they complain that they do not feel anything, so they quit. If they would be persistent, however, and continue diligently to cultivate the *fruit* of love toward the Father, then the *feeling* of love would eventually come.

One thing is certain—the true feelings associated with love will never come apart from the Father, for He *is* love.

Jesus recognized this truth at a very crucial time in His life when He did not feel like doing God's will. The place was the Garden of Gethsemane. Our Lord knew that God's will for His life was the cross. He knew that love was doing God's will. How did He react? What did He do?

> *And he went a little farther, and fell on his face, and prayed, saying,: O my Father, if it be possible, let this cup pass from me: nevertheless not as I will, but as thou wilt.*
>
> *Matthew 26:39*

Jesus expressed to the Father the ultimate expression of love of which man is capable. He had said earlier, "Greater love hath no man than this, that a man lay down his life for his friends" (John 15:13). In the same respect, there is no greater expression of love to the Father from His children than for them to cultivate the fruit of love toward Him by spending time in His Word, praying in the Spirit, and performing acts of love. For by so doing, they will be laying down their lives for their God.

May we believers begin the process of cultivation of love, so we will truly love God with all our heart, all our soul, and with all our mind. That is, after all, the first and greatest commandment (Matthew 22:37).

THE FORCE OF JOY

"But the fruit of the Spirit is...joy..."
Galatians 5:22

Of all the fruits of the Spirit of God, joy is the most important for an overcomer. At some time each of us experiences the sorrows, the pains, the agonies, the frustrations, and the condemnations that come with serving the Lord Jesus Christ. If we desire to conquer all these things, however, we must develop the fruit of joy, because the power to overcome is joy's main attribute.

> *Because thou servest not the Lord thy God with joyfulness, and with gladness of heart, for the abundance of all things; Therefore shalt thou serve thine enemies which the Lord shall send against thee, in hunger, and in thirst, and in nakedness, and in want of all things: and he shall put a yoke of iron upon they neck, until he have destroyed thee.*
> *Deuteronomy* 28:47, 47

These scriptures reveal the consequences of serving God

without joy. According to verse 48, the absence of joy in believers' lives results in their serving the enemy, wanting all things, and having a yoke of iron place upon their necks.

On the other hand, for those who do serve the Lord with joy and gladness of heart, the opposite will be true. They will overcome the enemy and experience fulfillment in all things and be free of the yoke of bondage. Thus there are three functions of the fruit of joy: 1) to produce victory, 2) to provide fulfillment, and 3) to protect against oppression.

When the fruit of joy is developed in the life of a believer, he will overcome the enemy. According to 2 Peter 2:19, whatever overcomes a person becomes his master: "while they promise them liberty, they themselves are the servants of corruptions: for of whom a man is overcome, of the same is he brought in bondage."

Whatever overcomes an individual becomes his master. People serve whatever they are in bondage to. Believers are no exception to this rule. Since whatever overcomes a person places him in bondage, and since whatever he is bound to he serves, then we can see why there are so many believers who are unconsciously bound to the enemy and are unwittingly serving him. In the same respect, however, if a believer is bound to the Lord Jesus, then he is serving God.

During times of trial, we believers can assess the degree to which we are in bondage to the enemy by measuring the extent to which our trials overcome us. This may be determined by examining our individual response to personal trials—but let each of us examine himself only.

For example, let a believer ask himself the following: "How do I respond when I must suffer through an extended illness? How do I react when the enemy stirs up my family or friends to persistently harass and persecute me? How do I bear up under lengthy trials as opposed to brief ones? How am I honestly conducting myself in the midst of the trials which I am experiencing right now?" The answers to these questions are very important, because if a believer's disposition or his character or even his countenance changes during the time of trial, then he is to some extent overcome by that trial.

According to 2 Peter 2:19, "...of whom a man is overcome, of the same is he brought in bondage." Believers who change during their trials are in danger of going into bondage to the enemy. Since the source of every trial is Satan, multitudes of believers are thus unknowingly serving the enemy during the time of their trials. These people may "be strong in the Lord, and in the power of His might" (Ephesians 6:10)—until they encounter a trial. Then they suddenly lose all their strength, for then their whole character, disposition, and countenance changes. They begin serving the enemy, for in faltering, they are in essence allowing themselves to be overcome by their trials. Admittedly, they may be ignorant of the servitude to Satan; nevertheless, it is true to a certain degree.

On the other hand, if a believer goes through a trial and others are unable to detect it, then despite his suffering, he is not in real bondage to the enemy because he has not allowed that trial to defeat him. There are not many believers today who overcome trials to the degree that their countenance or disposition does not betray their affliction. This is unfortunate, for such people are the few true overcomers in the Church today.

The reason there are so few real overcomers in the Church of Jesus Christ is because so few Christians have expended the effort necessary to cultivate and develop the fruit of joy in their individual lives. Joy is the strength that enables a person to remain "steadfast, unmovable, always abounding in the work of the Lord" (1 Corinthians 15:58). In essence, *joy is a preventative fruit that protects against falling into bondage and servitude to the enemy of God.*

The following scriptures reveal the response that God desires of His children during times of trial:

> *Beloved, think it not strange concerning the fiery trial which is to try you, as though some strange thing happened unto you: But rejoice, inasmuch as ye are partakers of Christ's suffering; that, when his glory shall be revealed, ye may be glad also with exceeding joy.*
> *1 Peter 4:12, 13*

God wants His children to rejoice even in times of trial. Since the flesh does not want to do this, the only way to be obedient to the will of God as expressed in 1 Peter 4:12, 13 is through the development of the fruit of joy.

Jesus Christ has not called His followers to be unstable. It is not His desire that they change during their trials. On the contrary, He wants stability in those who follow Him. His life set forth this example.

Jesus was tempted with everything that we believers are tempted with today. He went through trials of sickness, oppression, depression, and persecution; but His character and disposition never changed. His trials never even showed on His countenance. It is not recorded in scripture that any of his followers ever once looked at Jesus and asked, "What's the matter, Master? Have a rough day?" Jesus developed joy in His life so that it produced one-hundredfold fruit:

> *For consider him that endured such contradiction of sinners against himself, lest ye be wearied and faint in your minds. Ye have not yet resisted unto blood, striving against sin.*
>
> *Hebrews* 12:3, 4

Jesus perhaps experienced His greatest trial in the Garden of Gethsemane. He resisted giving in to this trial to the point that He sweat great drops of blood. He was striving against sin so much that He resisted unto blood. He overcame this trial and honored the Father's will. The source of the strength that enabled Him to overcome is revealed in Hebrews 12:2: "Looking unto Jesus the author and finisher of our faith; who for the joy that was set before him endured the cross, despising the shame, and is set down at the right hand of the throne of God."

It was joy which gave Jesus the strength to overcome and not serve the enemy.

Is there a believer today who has yet resisted unto blood in order to do the will of God? Most of us today must shamefully admit that, on the contrary, our faces have often been windows publicly spotlighting and displaying our trials for all to see. Yet, our trials are not even close to the magnitude of the trial that Jesus endured in the Garden. Through cultivating and developing the fruit of joy, however, we will gain strength to overcome the various trials of life, regardless of their magnitude or length. We believers are admonished in Hebrews 12:2 to look unto Jesus. Jesus overcame by the fruit of joy.

The second function of the fruit of joy is the production of all things necessary for abundant living. Those who cultivate and develop joy in their lives will experience fulfillment in *all* things:

> *My brethren, count it all joy when ye fall into diverse temptations; Knowing this, that the trying of your faith worketh patience. But let patience have her perfect work, that ye may be perfect and entire, wanting nothing.*
>
> *James 1:2–4*

The Greek word translated patience in verse three and four actually means "*endurance.*" So James 1:3, 4 could be read as follows: "Knowing this, that the trying of your faith worketh *endurance.* But let *endurance* have her perfect work, that ye may be perfect and entire, wanting nothing."

According to Nehemiah 8:10, the source of endurance is joy: "...for the joy of the Lord is your strength (your endurance)". We believers are going to endure our trials only as long as we are joyful, for the strength to endure simply is not present without joy.

There are three promises contained in James 1:4 for those believers who do endure their trials with joy: 1) They will be perfect, 2) they will be entire, and 3) they will want (lack) nothing. The promise of "wanting nothing" is the direct opposite of being in "want of all things" as noted in Deuteronomy 28:48. We Christians can actually reach a place in our lives where we can honestly and continually say with David: "The Lord is my shepherd; I shall not want" (Psalm 23:1). We will resist and overcome the enemy so much that we will have this testimony: "I am in need of nothing, for God is faithful; I do not lack any good thing."

There is no reason for any believer to ever live in lack of any good thing. There is nothing needful in life which our salvation does not abundantly supply. Peter tells us that God "hath given unto us all things that pertain unto life and godliness, through the knowledge of him that hath called us to glory and virtue" (2 Peter 1:3). The prophet Isaiah promises: "Therefore with joy shall ye draw water out of the wells of salvation" (Isaiah 12:3). Salvation means safety, soundness, deliverance, preservation, and health. It covers *every* aspect of life—not just the spiritual aspect.

A trial is an attempt by the enemy to steal something of value from a believer—whether it is finances or health or a loved one or any other good thing God desires for His children to have and enjoy. There is nothing the enemy can steal, however, that is not abundantly provided for in salvation. The condition for receiving the benefits of this salvation is an attitude of joy. Joy is the bucket that enables a person to scoop down into the wells of salvation and draw out whatever is lacking in his life. The wells of salvation contain such things as healing, financial prosperity, safety, preservation and soundness of body and mind. These blessings are drawn to the surface (or to manifestation) through joy. So if the enemy manages to steal a believer's joy, he has effectively stolen that person's access to the benefits of his salvation.

The third function of the fruit of joy is breaking of the yoke of iron on a believer's neck: "My brethren, count it all joy when ye fall into divers temptations" (James 1:2). Count it all joy is just as much a commandment as love thy neighbor. It is just as much a sin not to count it all joy during a trial as it is to hate a brother or sister in Christ. To count it all joy does not mean to praise God at the outset of a trial and then from that point on to act and look discouraged until the fulfillment of the need is manifested. It means to praise God and be joyful *throughout* the trial—from beginning to end.

Many believers are joyful over the short haul, but lack the strength and endurance to be joyful in long, drawn-out trials. They may begin with joy, but after a while that joy seems to wear thin. It's not long before it has disappeared entirely. Once this happens, the yoke of iron is immediately imposed upon their necks. It is then only a matter of time before they fall under the weight of it.

It is easy to detect when a Christian's joy is about to go during a trial because he will begin asking such questions as: "How much longer must I endure?" "Why me?" "Do you realize how long I have been standing in faith for an answer to this situation?" Questions such as these are a sure indication that joy is about to depart, for according to Proverbs 15:23, "A man hath joy by the answer of his moth: and a word spoken in due season, how good is it!" As soon as joy withers from the tongue, it begins to wither from the heart.

Joy is not based on feelings or circumstances; joy is bestowed by God and resides in one's spirit. Psalm 105:37 refers to God bringing Israel out of bondage in the land of Egypt: "He brought them forth also with silver and gold: and there was not one feeble person among their tribes." The Hebrew word translated feeble is a root word meaning "*to falter, stumble, faint or fall.*"

The source of these people's strength is revealed in Psalm 105:43: "And he brought forth his people with joy, and his chosen with gladness." God knew exactly what it would take to give His people strength to overcome the effect of their adverse circumstances. It took joy.

Trials of adverse circumstances are going to increase in the world for us believers as we see the day approaching (Hebrews 10:25). But we have the potential within our spirits not to be shaken by these approaching storms. Although circumstances will become increasingly adverse and more people will find themselves overcome by the cares of life, this need not happen to the children of God. However, if we believers have not learned how to overcome our present trials, if we are already being shaken by what we are experiencing today, then as the trials of life intensify we will find them much more difficult—if not impossible—to endure.

It will only be through the fruit of joy that we will have the ability to overcome the trials which lie ahead of us all. That's why it is imperative that we realize that the time to begin cultivating joy in our own lives is today.

Concerning that day of His coming, Jesus forewarned believers in Luke 21:34: "And take heed to yourselves, lest at any time your hearts be overcharged with surfeiting, and drunkenness, and cares of this life, and so that day come upon you unawares." The word translated surfeiting is *kraipale* (*krahee-pal'-ay*) and refers to overindulging as with food or drink. It also refers to the disgust or nausea that result from overindulgence.

This is the problem with many Christians today; they are "overcharged with surfeiting." They are drinking so much of the cup of the cares of this life that they are experiencing the discomfort brought on by living in a drunken, nauseated spiritual state. They are ignoring the Lord's warning to take heed to themselves. Their minds have become so saturated with the cares of life; they are so weary and drunken that they do not have ears to listen to what the Spirit is saying to the Church today. In addition, they are so nauseated with the trials of life that their vision is blurred so they are not even aware of the day and time in which they are living.

We believers need the fruit of joy in order to break the bondage of heaviness and to overcome the trials of life. Then we will have a sharp eye to see and clear mind to understand the signs of the times, as well as an open ear to hear what the Spirit is speaking to the Church in these last days. Then we will know what our Lord is asking of the Church and what He is commanding it to do and to be. As we perceive and take heed, we will be found ready at the coming of the Lord Jesus and will be delivered out of the "land of Egypt." Like Israel, we too will be brought forth with joy (Psalm 105:43).

Many believers, however, are not concerned about preparing themselves for the coming of Jesus. This unconcern is evidence of their spiritual ignorance and apathy, for if they were truly aware of the nearness of His coming, they would not be living as they are. They would be diligently preparing their hearts by spending more time on their knees and in the Word of God. They would be counting the cares and trials of this life for what they really are—wood, hay, and stubble (1 Corinthians 3:12). Instead of being concerned for these temporal things, they would be seeking after gold, silver, and precious stones (1 Corinthians 3:12)—things that will last for eternity.

As Christians, we should be cultivating the fruit of joy, for it is one such eternal thing. One way in which we can cultivate the fruit of joy in our individual lives is by developing our faith.

Most Christians can quote the familiar passage of scripture in Romans 10:17: "So then faith cometh by hearing, and hearing by the Word of God." Many, however, are not aware of the close relationship between joy, faith, and the Word. Jesus taught this principle to His disciples in John 15:11: "These things have I spoken unto you, that my joy might remain in you, and that your joy might be full." What He had spoken to them was the Word of God. The Apostle John, in turn, later wrote: "And these things write we unto you, that your joy may be full" (1 John 1:4).

The Old Testament also recognized this truth as recorded by David in Psalm 19:8: "The statutes of the Lord are right, rejoicing the heart..." According to Jeremiah 15:16, there is an inseparable relationship between how much Word is "eaten," or assimilated, and the joy which resides in the heart: "Thy words were found, and I did eat them; and thy word was unto me the joy and rejoicing of mine heart: for I am called by thy name, O Lord God of hosts."

An appropriate question for us to ask ourselves when we are lacking joy is: "How much time do I spend in the Word of God?" If the answer is little or no time, then we can regain our lost joy by increasing the amount and quality of the time we spend in the Word developing our faith.

"And having this confidence, I know that I shall abide and continue with you all for your furtherance and joy of faith" (Philippians 1:25). In this scripture, Paul states that there is joy in faith. Believers who cultivate faith by spending time in the Word will also be cultivating the fruit of joy. The three are inseparable, for not only does *faith* come by hearing, and hearing by the Word of God, but *joy* also come the same way.

Just as there is no faith outside of the Word of God, likewise there is no joy outside of faith. A believer of weak faith is an individual of weak joy; whereas a believer a strong faith is an individual of strong joy: "Not for that we have dominion over your faith, but are helpers of your joy: for by faith ye stand" (2 Corinthians 1:24). In other words, a Christian's faith will never rise above his joy, and his joy will never rise above his faith. Joy and faith stand together. When one is missing, the other will fall. Both faith and joy stand upon the solid foundation of the eternal Word of God.

The lives of many believers in the Church today testify to these truths. Those who have weak faith and little joy, spend a limited amount of quality time in God's Word. They are not able to count it all joy during their trials because they simply do not have the solid faith that, come what may, God *will* provide for their needs. If only these weak believers would be diligent about getting into the Word and increasing their faith, then they would have more joy and possess the necessary strength to overcome their trials. Then, when times of tribulation arise, they would view them through the eyes of faith. Trials and tribulations have no other effect upon truly strong believers than to make their hearts rejoice.

As long as Christians live in the realm of unbelief, they will never experience joy. Admittedly, they might experience occasional happiness, but there is a big difference between joy and happiness. Happiness is dependent upon circumstances, but joy is independent of all circumstances or situations. With joy in the heart, when trials come along the believer can declare boldly, "Praise God, for He is faithful. All my needs will be fully met!"

In John 15:11, we read these words of our Lord: "These things have I spoken unto you, that my joy might remain in you, and that your joy might be full." Notice that Jesus said my joy and your joy. If each of us believers would experience the combination of these two joys in our spirit, then absolutely no circumstance whatsoever could defeat us.

"Whom having not seen, ye love; in whom, through now ye see him not, yet believing, ye rejoice with joy unspeakable and full of glory" (1 Peter 1:8). Before we can experience joy, we must first believe. Faith precedes joy. Many people today are seeking the joy of the Lord yet trying to bypass their faith. That won't work. They must first saturate that seed of joy in their spirit with the Word of God, and as faith takes root in their heart; joy will rise to the surface. Since faith pleases God (Hebrews 11:6), then the spirits of those who desire to please Him rejoice at the presence of faith. It is such a joy to have faith!

The second way in which believers can cultivate the fruit of joy is by the giving of themselves to others. The Apostle Paul wrote that the people to whom he ministered determined his joy: "Yea, and if I be offered upon the sacrifice and service of your faith, I joy, and rejoice with you all" (Philippians 2:17). "For what is our hope, or joy, or crown of rejoicing? Are not even ye in the presence of our Lord Jesus Christ at his coming? For ye are our glory and joy" (1 Thessalonians 2:19, 20). Paul was saying that as he gave himself to the people in the Philippian and Thessalonian churches, he received joy.

Many believers today do not have joy simply because they are self-centered, and yet, self-centeredness is a natural tendency of the flesh for those who are going through trials. If we Christians would only learn to reach out and minister to someone else during our times of trial, then we would learn that self-pity can easily be turned into joy by simple act of the will: "And the Lord turned the captivity of Job, when he prayed for his friends..." (Job 42:10). Those of us who are being held captive by the bands of selfishness can be delivered if we will but follow the example of Job and minister to the needs of others.

Selfishness chokes out the fruit of joy, so we cannot experience true joy until we learn to minister to other people. Some believers are hindered by the misconception that ministering to people's needs can only be done from behind a pulpit, but this just simply is not true. Praying for people, blessing people, and delivering people may be done anywhere at anytime. Jesus sent the seventy disciples out for this very purpose, and they returned from their ministry assignment filled with joy: "And the seventy returned again with joy, saying, Lord, even the devils are subject unto us through thy name" (Luke 10:17). As we learn to offer ourselves as a sacrifice for other people's faith, then the fruit of joy will be cultivated and developed in our own individual lives. We will then begin to say with Paul, "I joy and rejoice with you all."

"He that goeth forth and weepeth, bearing precious seed, shall doubtless come again with rejoicing, bringing the sheaves with him" (Psalm 126:6). The key to receiving joy when going forth is to bear precious seed. We must not go forth and do our own thing; instead, our actions must be in strict accordance with the Word of God. God promises joy especially to those who minister peace and reconciliation when they go out: "Deceit is in the heart of them that imagine evil: but to the counselors of peace is joy" (Proverbs 12:20).

According to Psalm 126:6, believers who go forth and sow the Word of God (that precious seed which they bear) will return with real, genuine joy. True joy is that joy which enables a person to drop down his buckets and draw up whatever he may need from the wells of salvation. This is why the Word tells us to "pray one for another, that ye may be healed..." (James 5:16). Ministering to others will cultivate joy in the hearts of the ministers, enabling them to drop the bucket into their own individual well of salvation and draw up from it whatever will minister to their own personal need.

The life of John the Baptist in an example of selflessness cultivating joy:

John answered and said, a man can receive nothing, except it be given him from heaven. Ye yourselves bear me witness, that I said, I am not the Christ, but that I am sent before him. He that hath the bride is the bridegroom: but the friend of the bridegroom, which standeth and heareth him, rejoiceth greatly because of the bridegroom's voice: my joy therefore is fulfilled. He must increase, but I must decrease.

John 3:27–30

Verse 30 is the key to John's joy and the solution to the mystery of why joy is missing in the lives of many believers today. John said of Jesus, "He must increase, but I must decrease." Self smothers joy, so joy is missing in the lives of those who are living for self. As Jesus increases in their lives, however, believers will begin to experience more and more joy. This will come as they learn to minister to others, for love cannot help but decrease self. The fruit of joy is developed a little more each time self is given away.

The life of the Apostle Paul is also an example of selflessness cultivating joy:

And now, behold, I go bound in the spirit unto Jerusalem, not knowing the things that shall befall me there: Save that the Holy Ghost witnesseth in every city, saying that bonds and affliction abide me. But none of these things move me, neither count I my life dear unto myself, so that I might finish my course with joy, and the ministry, which I have received of the Lord Jesus, to testify the gospel of the grace of God.

Acts 20:22–24

It is only as we lose our lives, as Paul did, that we will possess joy. Paul said in Acts 20:24, "neither count I my life dear unto myself..." In other words, Paul decreased, and Jesus increased. Paul recorded the result this action would have upon his life in verse 24, "...so that I might finish my course with joy..."

We can measure the extent to which we have lost our lives by listening closely to the words coming out of our mouths. How often do we make reference to such things as *my* life, *my* possessions, *my* ministry, and *my* feelings? These are not just expressions; they are an indication that self has increased, for how unlike the words of Paul the Apostle and John the Baptist are they! Both Paul and John lost "their" lives, and they did so willingly—*with joy!*

There is only one reason why believers are not willing to cultivate this fruit and thus possess joy, and it has a direct relationship to their lack of willingness to lose their lives. The reason is this: *they have more affection for temporal blessings than eternal blessings.*

Joy is based 100% on eternal considerations. When trials occur in the temporal realm, they do not affect the eternal realm. For example, if a trial occurs in the area of a believer's finances, it has no effect whatsoever on his eternal riches. Therefore, if that particular person has his affections based 100% on the eternal, then it will not matter to him what happens in the temporal realm because his joy is not dependent upon momentary, fleeting circumstances. A believer today could even undergo trials of Job and say with him as he did of his God, "Though he slay me, yet will I trust in him" (Job 13:15).

Too many believers still have more affection for their lives than they do for Jesus. Every Christian should ponder this question during his time of trial: "Am I more concerned with what his trial has cost me than I am for my blessed Lord and Savior?" If the answer is yes, then that believer desperately needs to reassess his values and his commitment to the Lord. There is absolutely no trial on this earth that will change Jesus Christ, and it is in Him and Him alone that true joy is found.

The third way in which a believer can cultivate the fruit of joy is by seeking God's presence: "Thou wilt shew me the path of life: in thy presence is fullness of joy; at thy right hand there are pleasures evermore" (Psalm 16:11). In the presence of God may be found the fullness of joy:

> *Verily, verily, I say unto you, That ye shall weep and lament, but the world shall rejoice: and ye shall be sorrowful, but your sorrow shall be turned to joy. A woman when she is in travail hath sorrow, because her hour is come: but as soon as she is delivered of the child, she remembereth no more of the anguish, for joy that a man is born into the world. And ye now therefore have sorrow: but I will see you again, and your heart shall rejoice, and your joy no man taketh from you.*
>
> *John 16:20–22*

Just as sorrow flees from a woman in labor at the moment of the baby's birth, so does sorrow flee from a believer at the moment of the manifestation of his long-awaited miracle. When the miracle occurs, the sorrow is forgotten, for it has turned into joy.

We Christians still live in the flesh, so we are still tempted with sorrow—feelings of anguish, hurt and pain—and therefore are still tempted with giving up. All believers have wondered at one time or another, "When will this prayer ever be answered?" Still another day passes without the desired miracle being manifested, and as a result there is a feeling of sorrow. "When will the healing manifest itself?" Yet the symptoms grow worse, and there is sorrow. "When will the finances come through?" Yet the bills keep piling up, and there is sorrow. "When will the door of opportunity ever open for me?" Yet nothing seems to be moving forward, and there is sorrow.

All of us have wondered at times, "Will it be worth all this sorrow when the manifestation finally does occur?" Jesus said that it will be just as it is in childbirth, when the child comes, the sorrow leaves. Anguish cannot abide in the same heart as joy, so the sorrow will be remembered no more. Yes, it surely will be worth it all—once we behold that manifested miracle!

In John 16:22 Jesus told the apostles that their sorrow would flee when they saw Him again; that is they would experience joy in His presence. This is where we believers today will find our joy also, for in His presence is fullness of joy (Psalm 16:11).

Great is the Lord, and greatly to be praised in the city
of our God, in the mountain of his holiness. Beautiful
for situation, the joy of the whole earth, is mount Zion,
on the sides of the north, to city of the great King.

Psalm 48:1, 2

The joy of the whole earth, according to verse 2 of this passage, is Mount Zion. A believer's joy therefore, will be found in seeking Mount Zion, which is a type or symbol of God's presence of the Lord. The more diligently one seeks the presence of the Lord, the more joy he will possess; whereas the believer who seeks His presence haphazardly will be lacking in joy.

Three basic elements of how to seek God's presence maybe found in James 4:8: "Draw nigh to God, and he will draw night to you. Cleanse your hands, ye sinners; and purify your hearts, ye double minded."

The first way to seek God's presence is to draw near to Him simply by an act of the will. God's presence will not seek us; we must take the initiative and seek it. Many believers have a tendency to look at certain people in the Body of Christ who they know have experienced God's presence and think that this is some kind of special gift from God. On the contrary, no one ever experiences God's presence who has not paid the cost of seeking it. God is not selective. He does not bestow His presence upon some and deny it to others; instead He bestows His presence upon all those who, by an act of their will, draw nigh to Him.

Experiencing the presence of God is not a special gift or a calling or a matter of God's selectivity; it is for any believer who is willing to pay the cost involved in drawing near to Him. All believers may experience God's presence and thereby increase their joy.

The second way to seek God's presence is to cleanse the hands. Trying to seek God's presence with unconfessed sin in the life will prove to be frustrating because according to Isaiah 59:2 He will hide His face from the sinful person: "But your iniquities have separated between you and your God, and your sins have hid his face from you, that he will not hear."

Jesus Christ has made it easy for us to cleanse our hands before seeking God's presence. All it requires is asking for forgiveness, repenting of our sin, and appropriating the blood of Jesus. It is no different for us today than it was for the priests in the Old Testament who always had to look into the laver, see their own reflections, recognize their imperfections and impurities, and then wash themselves before entering God's presence in the Holy of Holies. (Exodus 30:17–21). The laver is a symbol of God's Word by which believers today must examine and judge themselves so that they may be made aware of their sins and ask forgiveness in accordance to 1 John 1:9, before attempting to enter the holy presence of God.

In addition, when we as believers meet as a local body, we should cleanse our hands individually prior to seeing God's presence collectively in the worship service, for He commands that His people lift up holy hands unto Him when they seek to enter into His presence (1 Timothy 2:8). Believers who put this principle into practice will discover that their joy will have increased at the conclusion of each church service. Even those who usually find attending church unenjoyable will soon discover that it is a joy to "lift up holy hands" as they actively seek the presence of God with others of "like precious faith" (2 Peter 1:1).

The third way to seek God's presence is to purify the heart. According to James 4:8, believers must not be double-minded, but they must seek God with their whole heart. Too often, we try to seek God's presence without giving Him our undivided attention. It is impossible to wholeheartedly seek His presence while cleaning the house or washing the car or worrying about the job ahead, for this is trying to seek Him with only a portion of one's attention. This is double-mindedness and only leads to frustration. Seeking the presence of God with a whole heart requires giving Him undivided attention.

The individual believer knows when he is praying and seeking God with a whole heart, just as he knows when he is doing so only to ease his conscience or only because his minister is constantly telling him he is supposed to. God also knows: "Be not deceived; God is not mocked: for whatsoever a man soweth, that shall he also reap" (Galatians 6:7). God looks on the heart, and He knows exactly how much of it is seeking Him. A whole heart will willingly pay the cost involved in seeking the presence of God, and, as a result, the whole heart will reap joy.

For thus saith the Lord, 'that after seventy years be

accomplished at Babylon I will visit you, and perform my good word toward you, in causing you to return to this place. For I know the thoughts that I think toward you, saith the Lord, thoughts of peace, and not of evil, to give you an expected end. Then shall ye call upon me, and ye shall go and pray unto me, and I will hearken unto you. And ye shall seek me, and find me, when ye shall search for me with all your heart. And I will be found of you, saith the Lord: and I will turn away your captivity, and I will gather you from all the nations, and from all the places whither I have driven you, saith the Lord; and I will bring you again into the place whence I caused you to be carried away captive.

Jeremiah 29:10–14

When a local body meets for the sole purpose of seeking God with a whole heart, then they will experience His presence in their midst in a miraculous way. It will never happen, however, as long as believers meet with divided interest. Israel found God in Babylon, the land of their captivity, when they searched for Him with all their heart. The manifestation of His presence always brings deliverance to His people. Believers must first learn to seek Him wholeheartedly at home, and then they will be comfortable seeking Him wholeheartedly with the other members of the body. Then the body of Christ as a whole will find joy in the deliverance that always accompanies the manifestation of His mighty presence.

God is waiting for His people to cultivate and develop the fruit of joy so that they may be overcomers and thus witnesses to those in the world. The more the fruit of joy is cultivated and developed, the plumper it will be so that more and more people will be able to share in its satisfying taste. May we strive therefore to develop this fruit, extending it to others, and joyfully declaring with the Psalmist of old, "O taste and see that the Lord is good" (Psalm 34:8).

SEE THAT YOUR HEART
NOT BE TROUBLED

"But the fruit of the Spirit is...peace... "
Galatians 5:22

Many believers do not realize that peace is a fruit of the Spirit and must be cultivated in order for it to become fully developed. Peace is not just a feeling that one experiences at salvation, assuring him that he has been born again; peace is a fruit whose functions are vital for anyone to live in the fullness of the Spirit of God.

And as he sat upon the Mount of Olives, the disciples came unto him privately, saying, "Tell us, when shall these things be? And what shall be the sign of thy coming, and of the end of the world?" And Jesus answered and said unto them, "Take heed that no man deceive you. For many shall come in my name, saying, I am Christ; and shall deceive you. And ye shall hear of wars and rumors of wars: see that ye be not troubled: for all these things must come to pass, but the end is not yet. For nation shall rise against nation, and kingdom against kingdom: and there

shall be famines, and pestilences, and earthquakes, in divers places. All these are the beginning of sorrows."
Matthew 24:3–8

The first function of the fruit of peace is to prevent the hearts of God's people from being troubled. There will be some things which will come upon the earth that we cannot pray, fast, or confess away. Jesus explained in Matthew 24:6 that certain things must happen. In Matthew 24:7, He listed these things that must come upon the earth. Luke's account expounds upon what Jesus mentioned in Matthew's gospel:

Then said he unto them, "Nation shall rise against nation, and kingdom against kingdom: And great earthquakes shall be in divers places, and famines, and pestilences; and fearful sights and great signs shall there be from heaven."
Luke 21:10, 11

These things will be so fearful that they will have the potential of literally frightening people to death (Luke 21:26). Believers who feel secure just because they are in a church but who are passively living for God, are not guaranteed that they will be immune from this fear.

Jesus said that all these things are the beginning of sorrows (Matthew 24:8). Sorrows in the Greek refers to birth pangs or travail. In other words, the earth is about to give birth to the Great Tribulation. These things that Jesus spoke of are the beginning of the travail of the earth.

Just as any woman who is in labor experiences pain before her child is born, this earth must also experience pain—the pain of earthquakes, famines, pestilences, and fearful sights—before it can give birth to the Tribulation.

In addition, a woman in travail knows that her child is about to be birthed when the pains become more intense and closer together. The same is true of the travail of the earth, for as the birth pangs of Luke 21:10, 11 occur more frequently and with greater intensity, we can be assured that the earth is just about to be delivered. One who is alert can detect through the media and events place around the globe that the birth pangs spoken of by Jesus are intensifying to a greater degree than ever before in history. Whereas, we used to read of these signs happening yearly or monthly, now we hear of earthquakes, famines, pestilences—and especially fear-producing events of violence—occurring daily throughout the world. People are beginning to notice this increase of death and destruction. Even non-believers are beginning to ask, "What is happening to our world?"

Jesus gave His followers only one commandment concerning these things that would begin to start happening in the earth: "...see that ye be not troubled" (Matthew 24:6). This is the responsibility of each individual believer, because essentially what Jesus said was, "See to it that *you* are not troubled." The Lord is not going to come down and automatically establish peace in the heart of the individual believer. Therefore, we

Christians must not wait on God to provide peace for us; we must take the initiative and individually cultivate the fruit of peace in our heart.

In John 14:27, just before He was to leave this earth, our Lord gave us the parting word: "Peace I leave with you, my peace I give unto you: not as the world giveth, give I unto you. Let not your heart be troubled, neither let it be afraid." The presence of peace then is the thing that will keep trouble out of our heart. Regardless of the extent to which the forces of hell come against us, we will not be troubled if we possess the peace of God. We need to recognize the urgency of cultivating the fruit of peace *now*, because as the birth pangs continue to intensify about us, peace will be our only means of preservation.

Paul has a word to say about the situation in Philippians 4:6, 7. He exhorts us:

> *Be careful for nothing; but in everything by prayer and supplication with thanksgiving let your requests be made known unto God. And the peace of God, which passeth all understanding, shall keep your hearts and minds through Christ Jesus.*

The Greek word translated *keep* in verse seven is *phroureo* (*froo-reh'-o*), a military term that means to keep with a military guard or garrison. Having the peace of God is the same as having a military troop guarding one's heart and mind against the enemy. The reason many believers are overcome by the numerous attacks of the enemy in these troublesome times is because they have let down their guard. In essence, the Word of God admonishes us in Philippians 4:7 and John 14:27: "Get your guard up, and see to it that you are not troubled." Once again we see that peace is the responsibility of the individual believer.

Christians today may identify with the story of Mary and Martha, for it contrasts the troubled believer with the believer who is at peace:

> *Now it came to pass, as they went, that he entered into a certain village: and a certain woman named Martha received him into her house. And she had a sister called Mary, which also sat at Jesus' feet, and heard his word. But Martha was cumbered about much serving, and came to him, and said, "Lord, dost thou not care that my sister hath left me to serve alone? Bid her therefore that she help me." And Jesus answered and said unto her, "Martha, Martha, thou art careful and troubled about many things: But one thing."*
>
> *Luke 10:38:42*

The first thing that happens to believers when they lack peace and are troubled in their hearts is that they begin to neglect the most necessary part of life—sitting at the feet of Jesus and hearing His word. Like many of us today, Martha was moving all around Jesus as she was busily serving Him, but her troubled heart kept her from experiencing the peace that was available simply by sitting down at His feet.

At times, peace can so fill a room that the people in

it can seemingly hear a pin drop. That is how it must be in the hearts and minds of believers today, if they are to hear the voice of God. Too often, Christians sit at the feet of Jesus to hear His word, but lack the self-discipline to persevere until they find that peace of mind and heart which is vital in order to his voice.

Sometimes when believers are troubled, their minds are screaming so loudly that even if God were shouting instructions to them, they would be incapable of hearing Him. God speaks in a still, small voice (1 Kings 19:11, 12). So when we take the time and diligently put forth the effort to sit quietly and calmly at the feet of Jesus, He will be faithful to flood our troubled minds with peace, that we may hear the words He has especially for us.

Secondly, when the hearts of believers are troubled, many times they try to substitute serving the Lord for sitting at His feet. Often, they become irritated at those who are peacefully sitting with Jesus, just as Martha became vexed with Mary. Some Christians today actually become upset with other believers who do not worry as they do. They will even ask them regarding some distressing circumstance, "Don't you care?" The truth is that in order to be totally honest, many believers would have to answer, "No." The reason they don't "care" (worry) is because they have been sitting at the feet of Jesus and have cast all their cares upon Him (1 Peter 5:7).

Another familiar comment that troubled believers will make to believers with peace is, "Well, the least you can do is *look* concerned!" When one has been looking into the face of Jesus, however, his countenance cannot help but reflect His peace, making it difficult even to "look concerned."

The second function of the fruit of peace is to determine direction in the life of the earnest believer: "And let the peace of God rule in your hearts, to which also ye are called in one body; and be ye thankful" (Colossians 3:15). Once again, it is the responsibility of the individual believer to "let" peace rule in his heart, for peace must be developed by an act of the will and through practice. The Greek word translated rule in this verse is *brabeuo* (*brab-yoo'-o*), meaning "to act as an umpire, to arbitrate, decide." In other words, the peace of God will be a deciding factor in a believer's heart. As he cultivates the fruit of peace, it will keep him safe within the boundaries of God's will. Just as an umpire blows the whistle when a player steps out of bounds, so will the peace of God lift when a believer steps out of God's will for his life.

The peace of God's will acts as an umpire, so we need to learn to resist the easy temptation of jumping ahead of God and going on without His peace. We must learn to listen to our heart and detect whether or not we are peaceful concerning the decision that is about to be made. We will become better able to perceive the leading of His Spirit.

Many believers are trying to discern God's direction for their lives by attempting to hear His voice. They are even listening for a specific word of direction; yet they are frustrated in their efforts. God does speak to His people, and one very beautiful manner in which He does so is through the inner "umpire" of His peace, which He has placed within the heart of every believer. Those who are frustrated, yet so desirous of hearing God's voice, should first learn to follow the leading of His peace.

They should be aware, however, that this is a growth process. They will have to learn to resist the doubt and discouragement which may come if they attempt to follow this leading and still miss God's will. Continued effort will result in eventual success: "And let us not be weary in well doing: for in due season we shall reap, if we faint not" (Galatians 6:9).

God will also use the fruit of peace to keep His children within the boundaries of His divine protection. For example, it may be that many automobile accidents involving believers could have been avoided had those involved only been sensitive enough to follow the leading of the peace in their hearts.

Jesus said: "The thief cometh not, but for to steal, and to kill, and to destroy: I am come that they might have life, and that they might have it more abundantly" (John 10:10). The fruit of peace is one by which God desires to protect His people.

The third function of the fruit of peace is to enable believers to be peacemakers. We can only give to others that which we possess ourselves. Wise Solomon counseled us: "Keep thy heart with all diligence; for out of it are the issues of life" (Proverbs 4:23). Whatever is in the hearts of people will be manifested in their treatment of one another. Believers who are irritable, moody, and rude in their actions toward others are that way because their hearts are wrong. In the same respect, believers who cultivate the fruit of peace in their hearts will find themselves in the position of being peacemakers, simply because the peace they possess in their hearts will be manifested in its distribution to others.

The life of Jesus is a perfect example of the principle found in Proverbs 4:23. In Isaiah 9:6, one of his names is "The Prince of Peace", which must mean that His heart abounded with peace, enabling Him to minister peace to all those with whom He came in contact.

> *But now in Christ Jesus ye who sometimes were far off are made night by the blood of Christ. For he is our peace, who hath made both one, and hath broken down the middle wall of partition between us; And came and preached peace to you which were afar off, and to them that were nigh.*
>
> *Ephesians* 2:13, 14, 17

"Blessed are the peacemakers: for they shall be called the children of God" (Matthew 5:9). The reason peacemakers are blessed is because they are the children of God. Yet many believers are not aware of this biblical identification between the two. They do not realize that if they are to be called the children of God, being peacemakers is not an option. We believers must cultivate the fruit of peace so that we may minister peace to others, thus making them into peacemakers and thereby qualifying them to be called (recognized as) His children.

The Greek word for children in Matthew 5:9 is

actually *huios* (hwee-os') which means "son." It denotes the relationship of an offspring to its parent, with the emphasis upon the nature of the parent being evident in the child. Our heavenly Father desires that His children develop into peacemakers, the mature sons of God, those who are recognized as His offspring by their God-like natures and qualities. One of the most identifiable of these qualities is peace.

In Hebrews 12:14 we are told to "follow peace with all men, and holiness, without which no man shall see the Lord." People who are not peacemakers will not see the Lord, for this is a clear indication that they are not truly the sons of God nor joint-heirs with the Prince of Peace. All true believers in Christ have at least a seed of peace in their hearts. If they desire to see their Lord, then it is of the utmost importance that they cultivate and develop the fruit of peace He has placed in their lives.

One characteristic of peacemakers is their nonresistance to evil. Too many Christians, however, are always concerned that they obtain their rights, express *their* opinions, and take whatever actions they feel are justified in the every situation that arises against *them*. The following "eye-for-an-eye" statements are representative of those prevalent in the Body of Christ today and are sometimes even taught as acceptable attitudes for the child of God: "You hurt me, and I'll hurt you back. You cost me something by your actions, and I'll sue you to get back what you owe me. You wrong me, and I'll make you suffer for it. You kill my dog, and I'll kill your cat."

As a result of a lack of proper teaching in the Church, there is often little discernable difference today between Christians and non-Christians, concerning this matter of repaying evil for evil. This sad situation has caused the fruit of peace to wither among the pews. As a teaching of non-resistance to evil is re-established in the Church, however, it will create an atmosphere in which the fruit of peace will flourish and out of which true peacemakers will arise.

This renewal must occur in the Body of Christ today, because our recognition by the world as the sons of God is dependent upon it. According to Romans 8:19 the day of our manifestation is drawing nigh; there is no time to waste. We Christians must be making ourselves known. We do that by our attitudes and actions. This troubled world will easily recognize peacemakers as the children of God, just as Pilate marveled greatly as the non-resistance of Jesus to His crucifixion (Matthew 27:14). The end result of returning good for evil—of suffering injustice without murmuring or retaliation—is that it makes it evident to the whole world which of its inhabitants are truly the sons of God (1 Peter 2:20; Matthew 27:54).

Ye hath heard that it hath been said, An eye for an eye, and a tooth for a tooth: But I say unto you, That ye resist not evil: but whosoever shall smite thee on thy right cheek, turn to him the other also. And if any man will sue thee at the law, and take away thy coat, let him have thy cloak also. And whosoever shall compel thee to go a mile, go with him twain.

Give to him that asketh thee, and from him that would borrow of thee turn not thou away.

Matthew 5:38–42

Jesus clearly stated that the law of retaliation permitted under the Mosaic dispensation is abolished under the dispensation of grace. Jesus instituted the "law of love" when He taught, "Resist not evil" (Matthew 5:39). Believers today should respond to evil only with acts of love. It is no longer "an eye for an eye, and a tooth for a tooth," but rather it is a kind word for malicious slander or a charitable response for an evil action or a willingness to freely give up possessions that are taken away by force. It is the love of God given to undeserving people. In essence, it is *grace.*

Dearly beloved, avenge not yourselves, but rather give place unto wrath: for it is written, Vengeance is mine; I will repay, saith the Lord. Therefore if thine enemy hunger, feed him; if he thirst, give him drink: for in so doing thou shalt heap coals of fire on his head. But not overcome of evil, but overcome evil with good.

Romans 12:19–21

The Greek word translated avenge is *ekdikeo* (*ek-dik-eh'-o*) meaning to inflict pain or harm in return for pain or harm inflicted on oneself. According to this passage of scripture, God does not want His children to attempt to extract their "pound of flesh" by punishing those who have wronged them. This does not mean, however, that there are not some who deserve to be punished.

It just means that it is not our place to dole out that punishment: "Vengeance is mine; I will repay" (v. 19). It means that God wants His children to remain in the role of peacemakers and not to infringe upon His role as avenger.

Too many believers try to play God. We can avoid this dangerous snare by always being careful to minister love, peace, and reconciliation to our enemies, leaving vengeance and retaliation to the Lord to whom it rightfully belongs.

Only as we cultivate and develop the fruit of peace will we be capable of living as the true sons of God. As soon as we try to "fight our won battles" we lose our peace, thus opening the door for a spirit of retaliation to come in. If we fall into this trap of the enemy, we will soon find ourselves driven to continually returning evil for evil. The end result will be disastrous.

After Peter attempted to defend Jesus by slicing off the ear of one of the men who came to arrest Him in the Garden of Gethsemane, Jesus said to him: "Put up again thy sword into his place: for all they that take the sword shall perish with the sword" (Matthew 26:52). Today, Jesus is still telling His disciples the same thing: "Put away the sword of retaliation, lest it be used against you." Instead, He desires that we follow His example: "And Jesus answered and said, Suffer ye thus far. And he touched his ear, and healed him" (Luke 22:51).

But I say unto you, Love your enemies, bless them that curse you, do good to them that hate you, and pray for them which despitefully use you, and persecute you;

That ye may be the children of your Father which is in heaven: for he maketh his sun to rise on the evil and on the good, and sendeth rain on the just and on the unjust.

Matthew 5:44–45

Only as we cultivate and develop the fruit of peace will we have the strength to bestow love, blessings, kindnesses, and prayers upon those who either outwardly or subtly resist us with evil. Obeying this particular teaching of Jesus will make us overcomers so that we may be the children of our Father which is in heaven (Matthew 5:45). It is for this reason that peacemakers are blessed, because they *are* the children of God.

Prayer is one way to cultivate the fruit of peace in our individual lives:

Be careful for nothing; but in every thing by prayer and supplication with thanksgiving let your requests be made known unto God. And the peace of God, which passeth all understanding, shall keep your hearts and minds through Christ Jesus.

Philippians 4:6, 7

Prayer produces the peace of God. There are those however, who pray about situations but are still troubled when they rise from their knees. The reason for this is that they neglect to include the condition for peace in their prayer: thanksgiving. The peace will come during the praise, the worship, and the expressions of appreciation that God has heard and answered in the prayer just offered. Prayer and supplication alone will not bring peace to the heart, but prayer and supplication *with thanksgiving* will open the way for the peace of God that will guard the heart and mind as though they were encircled by a military garrison.

"I create the fruit of the lips; Peace, peace to him that is far off, and to him that is near, saith the Lord; and I will heal him" (Isaiah 57:19). The fruit of the lips brings peace. According to Hebrews 13:15, that "fruit" is a continual sacrifice of praise: "By him therefore let us offer the sacrifice of praise to God continually, that is, the fruit of our lips giving thanks to his name."

The writing of the Apostle Paul reveals to us one way to give thanks which is pleasing to God:

> For if I pray in an unknown tongue, my spirit prayeth, but my understanding is unfruitful. What is it then? I will pray with the spirit, and I will pray with the understanding also: I will sing with the spirit and I will sing with the understanding also. Else when thou shalt bless with the spirit, how shall he that occupieth the room of the unlearned say Amen at thy giving of thanks, seeing he understandeth not what thou sayest? For thou verily givest thanks well, but the other is not edified.
>
> *1 Corinthians 14:14–17*

Believers who pray in tongues are praying "with the spirit" (vv. 14, 15). Verse 15 differentiates between praying "with the spirit" and praying "with the understanding." According to verse 16, praying with the spirit is a means of giving thanks, and according to verse 17 it is the giving of thanks "well." Therefore, as we make our prayers and supplication to God with our understanding, we would do well to also offer them with our spirit. The result would be that we would experience more of the peace of God, and that peace would become more developed in our individual lives. We should practice this dual type of praying and worshipping so consistently that we will not consider any prayer or supplication fully complete unless it has produced peace in the heart. When that happens, then we can honestly and assuredly conclude our prayer by declaring, "Amen; so be it!"

There are two topics that believers are commanded to pray for by the Apostle Paul in 1 Timothy 2:1, 2. Anyone who prays for these two "things" can be assured that he is offering up "peace-producing" prayers. The first is found in verse 1: "I exhort therefore, that, if first of all, supplications, prayers, intercessions, and giving of thanks, be made for all men."

It is possible that many of our prayers are hindered because we believers are not praying for what God commanded us to pray for, in order of His established priority. One reason many believers are not living in peaceful circumstances is because they have not been observing God's divine order that prayers be made "first of all...for all men" (v. 1).

"All men" is a very inclusive group. It would include those who do not agree with us, as well as those who share our viewpoints and opinions; those who oppose and demean us, as well as those who esteem and admire us; our enemies and those who persecute and despitefully use us, as well as our friends and family members; those who cannot or will not return our love and respect, as well as those who do.

First Timothy 2:2 contains the second prayer directive with a promised result of peace: "For kings, and for all that are in authority; that we may lead a quiet and peaceable life in all godliness and honesty." Those who obey the Word of the Lord and place priority on praying for their political and spiritual leaders will cultivate the fruit of peace that will be manifested in the circumstances surrounding their daily lives. Their hearts will be more filled with peace because of their obedience to God's commandment.

This truth is brought forth in Psalm 122:6, 7 in which the Psalmist exhorted the people of his day: "Pray for the peace of Jerusalem: they shall prosper that love thee. Peace be within thy walls, and prosperity within thy palaces." It is unexplainable to the carnal mind, but it is a spiritual principle that those who pray for the peace of "Jerusalem" (the seat of their Church and their government) will experience peace within their walls.

But this is not the end of our obligation and responsibility. In the Old Testament, the children of Israel were instructed to pray for "Jerusalem"; that is their *own* nation and people. Later, in the New Testament, this injunction was interpreted and modified by the Lord Jesus Christ when He taught His followers:

Ye have heard that it hath been said, Thou shalt love

thy neighbor, and hate thine enemy. But I say unto you, Love your enemies, bless them that curse you, do good to them that hate you, and pray for them which despitefully use you, and persecute you; That ye may be the children of your Father which is in heaven.

Matthew 5:43–45

The Greek word translated children in verse 45 is *huios*— "sons." Our Lord commanded that we not only pray for the peace of our own nation and people and allies, but also that we pray for our enemies—political, as well as spiritual. The manner in which we Christians treat our enemies is one of the most important indicators of our "sonship"—our God-likeness: "...for he maketh his sun to rise on the evil and on the good, and sendeth rain on the just and the unjust...Be ye therefore perfect, even as your Father which is in heaven is perfect" (vv. 45, 48).

Being like their heavenly Father produces peace in the hearts of His children, His *sons.* One way in which we can be like our Father is by praying for our enemies, even as Jesus prayed for those who crucified Him.

Abide in me, and I in you. As the branch cannot bear fruit of itself, except it abide in the vine; no more can ye, except ye abide in me. I am the vine, ye are the branches: he that abideth in me, and I in him, the same bringeth forth much fruit: for without me ye can do nothing.

John 15:4, 5

Abiding in Jesus is the second way in which believers may cultivate the fruit of peace in their individual lives. To *abide* means to permanently dwell; to make a homestead; to continue. Abiding in Christ, therefore, does not mean coming in and going out of His presence at one's own personal convenience; it means to *remain* continually in that presence regardless of one's feelings or circumstances.

Jesus said that those who abide in Him would bring forth much fruit. One of these fruits is peace: these things I have "spoken unto you, that in me ye might have peace. In the world ye shall have tribulation: but be of good cheer; I have overcome the world" (John 16:33). There is much peace to be found in abiding in the Lord. Ultimately we will find peace only in Him. It is by continually abiding in the presence of God that we will experience His peace in our hearts.

One definition of *peace* is "a state of security." There is no greater sense of security to be found anywhere other than in the presence of Jesus. Insecurity in the lives of believers is a direct result of not abiding in Him. Therefore, the remedy for insecurity is abiding in His presence because only such an atmosphere is conducive to producing the fruit of peace.

> *But, behold, the hand of him that betrayeth me is with me on the table. And truly the Son of man goeth, as it was determined: but woe unto that man by whom he is betrayed! And they began to inquire among themselves, which of them it was that should do this thing.*
>
> *Luke* 22:21, 23

When Jesus announced to the twelve disciples that one of them would betray Him, they revealed their insecurities by sorrowfully asking, "Lord is it I?" (Matthew 26:22). They had been with Jesus for three years, but were not secure in the fact that they would be faithful to Him.

In the same respect, many of His disciples today reveal their insecurities when they are faced with the possibility that they might fall away if they are not careful. They may feel secure in the knowledge of their eternal salvation through such teaching as "once saved, always saved," but their insecurities may manifest themselves through various attitudes and critical remarks they make toward teachings that deal with the need for maturing in the Lord.

The reason many believers religiously reject teaching that places individual responsibility on them is because they are continually asking themselves, "Will I be able to live up to what I am supposed to be as a Christian?" In their own way, such people are just as insecure about their faithfulness to the Lord as were the twelve disciples who asked Him, "Lord, is it I?"

God wants His children to be secure in Him, so that when they hear the Word that demands of them a decision; there will be no question whatsoever in their minds about whether or not they will overcome. He wants His sons to be as sure of their faithfulness to Him as they are of His faithfulness to them. He desires that they be so secure in their knowledge of Him and His will that when they are brought face to face with a spiritual crossroads, they will not ask themselves, "Will I be faithful?" but rather will confidently state, "Praise God, I have received this truth from the Word of God; therefore I will do it!"

According to Luke 22:24, the reason the twelve disciples expressed insecurity when Jesus revealed that one of them was a traitor was because they were still living for self: "And there was also a strife among them, which of them should be accounted the greatest." This is also the reason His disciples today are insecure. Many are still resisting the will of God for their lives because they have not died to self. As a result, they are troubled and insecure.

Jesus said, "He that findeth his life shall lose it: and he that loseth his life for my sake shall find it" (Matthew 10:39). Believers find the freedom to live when they die to self because peace and security in Jesus come only when self has been dethroned and Christ installed in its place.

True peace may be found when one reaches the point that they no longer resist the will of God. We can determine how much we are resisting God by determining how many of the truths in the Word we are obeying as they are revealed to us by the Holy Spirit.

For example, as God reveals to us that we need to fast more often, do we fast? As the Lord makes known to us that we need to be more diligent in prayer, do we begin to pray more? As we come to realize that there are bad habits in our lives that we need to overcome, do we promptly set about to take dominion over them? As the

Word of God is being ministered and we are made aware of new truth which affects our attitude and behavior, do we squirm in our seat, or do we pray, "Lord, show me what I need to do to apply this truth to my own life?"

Those who are resisting God's will for their lives will struggle with such thoughts as: "I can't do that. What would people think? What would it cost me?" They will only find peace when they come to the place where obeying God's Word is no longer a struggle but a joy.

As believers, all of us have some type of ministry—whether large or small. Fear of failure is an indication of striving for self. It will lead to struggling with self-efforts to open doors that assure success. This is the reason so many ministries operate in the flesh—the people involved have a fear of failure which leads to their producing an "Ishmael" (a product of their fleshy effort) that will later rise up and persecute their "Isaac" (work performed solely by the Spirit of God).

This was exactly what happened in the life of Abraham. His fear of failure caused him to rely on his own efforts, which produced Ishmael, his *child of the flesh,* who later rose up and persecuted Isaac, his *child of the Spirit* (Genesis 21:9, 10). As we, who are involved in ministry, admit that we were failures from the moment of our birth, give up trust in our own efforts, and allow God to be God, then we will find peace: "Thou wilt keep him in perfect peace, whose mind is stayed on thee: because he trusteth in thee" (Isaiah 26:3).

There is also the danger of striving for self in our personal lives. The attitude indicated by the expressions "*my* family," *my* life," "*my* possessions," "*my* desires" indicates that individually we have not died to self. Those who have truly died to self will obey the Word of God regardless of the degree to which it conflicts with their lives. They will possess an attitude of prompt and joyful obedience.

For example, when faced with fleshly desires, the truly obedient believer will be quick to respond to the scriptural admonition expressed by the Apostle Paul in Romans 12:1: "I beseech you therefore, brethren, by the mercies of God, that ye present your bodies a living sacrifice, holy, acceptable unto God, which is your reasonable service."

Believers who have died to self will also rejoice at obeying Christ's injunction found in Luke 9:23: "...If any man will come after me, let him deny himself, and take up his cross daily, and follow me." They will gladly take up their cross and follow Him, for they know that by so doing, they will find His peace.

Loving the Word of the Lord is the third way in which believers may cultivate the fruit of peace in their individual lives. The Psalmist says of his God: "Great peace have they which love thy law: and nothing shall offend them" (Psalm 119:165). To love the Word of the Lord is to love the Lord Himself—and vice versa.

In John 14:21, Jesus gave us an indicator by which we can measure the degree of our love for Him: "He that hath my commandments, and keepeth them, he it is that loveth me..." Therefore, love of the Lord is not indicated by memorizing Scripture verses, constantly studying the Bible, preaching the Gospel to others, or hungering after Bible teaching. Love of the Lord is indicated by keeping His words:

> *Jesus answered and said unto them, "If a man love me, he will keep my words: and my Father will love him, and we will come unto him, and make our abode with him. He that loveth me not keepeth not my sayings: and the word which ye hear is not mine, but the Father's which sent me."*
>
> *John 14:23, 24*

We believers may hear the Word of the Lord, receive it, and learn it—but we will not receive peace until we have learned to keep it: "Those things, which ye have both learned, and received, and heard, and seen in me, do: and the God of peace shall be with you" (Philippians 4:9).

> *Thus saith the Lord, thy Redeemer, the Holy One of Israel; I am the Lord thy God which teacheth thee to profit, which leadeth thee by the way that thou shouldest go. O that thou hadst hearkened to my commandments! Then had thy peace been as a river, and thy righteousness as the waves of the sea.*
>
> *Isaiah 48:17, 18*

We will experience the peace of God flowing like a river in our lives when we take heed and keep His Word. Proverbs 3:1, 2 also promises peace to those who keep God's commandments: "My son, forget not my law; but let thine heart keep my commandments: For length of days, and long life, and peace, shall they add to thee." Believers who lack peace in their hearts should examine themselves to see if they are doing what they know to do of God's Word, for it may be that they have allowed themselves to forget.

In John 14:27 Jesus admitted that the world has a type of peace to offer people. According to Revelation 6:4, however, every semblance of peace will be taken from the earth. The world can only offer its inhabitants an unstable, short-lived, doomed substitute for true, lasting peace.

The child of God, on the other hand, is promised peace in his house (1 Kings 22:17), peace in the land (Leviticus 26:6), peace in the grave (2 Kings 22:20), peace in prosperity (1 Samuel 25:6), peace in the end (Psalm 37:37), peace in mind (Philippians 4:7), peace in his soul (Psalm 55:18), peace in his heart (Philippians 4:7), peace in abundance (Psalm 72:7), peace in his border (Psalm 147:4), peace in his children (Isaiah 54:13), and peace throughout eternity (1 Kings 2:33).

The child of God lives in peace (2 Corinthians 13:11); and as he lives, he lied down in peace (Psalm 4:8), sleeps in peace (Psalm 4:8), sows in peace (James 3:18), follows in peace (Hebrews 12:14), comes in peace (Genesis 28:21), departs in peace (James 2:16), seeks peace (1 Peter 3:11), and preaches peace (Acts 10:36).

He experiences perfect peace (Isaiah 26:3), great peace (Psalm 119: 165), multiplied peace (2 Peter 1:2), peace within (Psalm 122:8), peace with his enemies (Proverbs

16:7), peace with his brethren (1 Thessalonians 5:13), peace with his God (Numbers 25:12), and peace beyond understanding (Philippians 4:7)—all of which are made possible by the Prince of Peace (Isaiah 9:6): "but he was wounded for our transgressions, he was bruised for our iniquities: the chastisement of our peace was upon him; and with his stripes we are healed" (Isaiah 53:3).

STAND UP UNDER PRESSURE, PERSECUTION OR DISTRESS

"But the fruit of the Spirit is... longsuffering..."
Galatians 5:22

The word longsuffering means: "to suffer long; to gird up under pressure, persecution, distress, and trouble; to remain steadfast; patience."

Because many believers are trying to be led by the Spirit of God without being willing to suffer in the flesh, their lives are silently witnessing to the world that being a Christian is great—*as long as things are going well.* However, as soon as things begin to go wrong, the attitudes and actions of these people often present a totally different picture of Christianity. Yet it is precisely those times of personal suffering that are often the most effective witness to the world, for it is then that unbelievers can best see the difference that knowing the Lord makes in the life of an individual.

When the world sees someone who can come through his sufferings with faith, hope, and love; someone who can display the nature an attitude of God despite difficulty and suffering; someone who can emerge victorious from every conflict, they will stop, look, and listen to that person as though Jesus, Himself, were speaking to them. Therefore, if we believers are to be effective witnesses of the Lord Jesus Christ, it is imperative that we manifest the character of Jesus to the world. In order to do that, we desperately need the presence of the fruit of longsuffering in our individual lives.

The first function of the fruit of longsuffering is to produce endurance. We can define endurance as "the capacity to remain firm under suffering without yielding to anger, resentment, despair, or self-pity." The writer of Hebrews was referring to this attribute of endurance when he likened the Christian life to a foot race:

> *Wherefore seeing we also are compassed about with so great a cloud of witnesses, let us lay aside every weight, and the sin which doth so easily beset us, and let us run with patience the race that is set before us.*
>
> *Hebrews* 12:1

God has called us to run our race with patient endurance. That means that it is not a short sprint requiring great speed. Instead, this is the long, grueling type of race that demands endurance. Believers who run according to their feelings and emotions will never endure long enough to cross the finish line. Marathon runners would never finish their course if they stopped running as soon as they began to feel hot, thirsty, or tired. Yet so many times, we believers feel justified when we stop running at the appearance of the first drop of spiritual "sweat." We seem to individually reason, "Surely God doesn't expect me to run this race if it's going to cause me to *perspire!*"

The Apostle Paul is a perfect example of how to run the Christian race with endurance. In 2 Corinthians 11:23–28 he testified of what he was called upon to endure in order to finish the course set before him. He endured being beaten with whips and rods; he endured the weariness of hard travel; he endured the suffering inflicted by robbers, by his own countrymen, by the heathen, and by the hypocrites; he endured danger in the city, in the wilderness, and in the sea; he endured pain, imprisonment, shipwreck and physical discomfort; he endured the cares involved in being the overseer of all adverse circumstances. But Paul never gave up; he continued to run with patience the race that was set before him.

Why did Paul continue to persevere in the face of such suffering and opposition? He saw past the hardships of the race to the prize which awaited him at the finish line. Paul allowed nothing to deter him from reaching the goal and reward which lay before him.

We believers would do well to learn a lesson from the Apostle Paul. We should not take lightly the admonition of Hebrews 12:1 to run *our* race with patient endurance.

I have fought a good fight, I have finished my course, I have kept the faith: Henceforth, there is laid up for me a crown of righteousness, which the Lord, the righteous judge, shall give me at the day: and not to me only. But unto all them also that love his appearing.

2 Timothy 4:7, 8

All those who have been born again have crossed the starting line, but the crown of righteousness will be awarded only to those who endure to the finish. No consolation prizes will be given to those who start but only run for a limited time—whether days or years—and then drop out of the race: "And let us not be weary in well doing: for in due season we shall reap, if we faint not" (Galatians 6:9).

Unfortunately, in any given service of any local body, the odds are unfavorable that *every* person sitting in the congregation will still be living for Jesus a year later. The reason is that not everyone will run the race with endurance. Many think that all they must do to live for Jesus is walk an aisle, accept Him as Savior and Lord, and then sit back and relax for the rest of their lives. They seem to think that two steps across the starting line is enough to assure them a winner's wreath. They seem to expect somehow to be translated supernaturally to the finish line where they will receive their crown of righteousness.

However, Jesus said, "But he that shall endure unto the end, the same shall be saved" (Matthew 24:13). These words are repeated in Matthew 10:22 and Mark 13:13. Obviously, our Lord wants His followers to realize the importance of endurance.

In the sixth chapter of the Gospel of John, Jesus gained a large following after He fed the multitude of five thousand. He met the need they had, in the flesh, when He fed them the loaves and fish, but spiritually He refused to continue to feed their flesh indefinitely and unconditionally. He demanded of them a commitment which they considered too restraining. Therefore, many of them chose to drop out of the race when they heard His demands because they wanted to run the course on their own terms.

Many therefore of his disciples, when they had heard this, said, This is a hard saying; who can hear it? When Jesus knew in himself that his disciples murmured at it, he said unto them, Doth this offend you? From that time many of his disciples went back and walked no more with him.

John 6:60, 61, 66

The twelve, however, stayed with Him. It was to them He later said: "Ye are they which have continued with me in my temptations. And I appoint unto you a kingdom, as my Father has appointed unto me" (Luke 22:28, 29). The same will be true of believers today. Jesus referred to the signs of His coming and of the end of this age in the twenty-first chapter of Luke The signs He listed in verse 8–11 of that chapter are classified in Matthew 24:4–8 as the beginning of sorrows. The signs of Luke 21:12–19, however, will occur even before the beginning of sorrows:

But before all these, they shall lay their hands on you, and persecute you, delivering you up to the synagogues, and into prisons, being brought before kings and rulers for my name's sake... And ye shall be betrayed

by parents, and brethren, and kinfolks, and friends;
and some of you shall they cause to be put to death.
And ye shall be hated of all men for my name's sake.

Luke 21:12, 16, 17

These affliction and persecutions will cause some to drop out of the race, but those who have developed the fruit of longsuffering will remain firm without yielding to adverse circumstances. Jesus attested to the importance of endurance for believers living during the fulfillment of these signs when He said: "In your patience possess ye your souls" (Luke 21:19).

Many Christians cannot comprehend having to endure more than what they are presently enduring. They are even now individually crying out to God, "Lord, I can't handle any more. Just one more thing and I'll be forced to give up the race."

In the Old Testament, Jeremiah had this reaction to the situations he was forced to face (which were similar to the situations believers must face in the end time). In Jeremiah 12:1–4, he cried out to God and said in essence, Lord, I can't handle any more. I'm at the end of my rope. God's response to Jeremiah was: "If thou hast run with the footmen, and they have wearied thee, then how canst thou contend with horses? And if in the land of peace, wherein thou trustest, they wearied thee, then how wilt thou do in the swelling of Jordan?" (Jeremiah 12:5). In other words, God said, "Cheer up, Jeremiah. Things are going to get worse!"

God did not promise us believers a trouble-free existence in these last days; instead, He has warned us in His Word about future affliction and persecution. So to those who are even now crying out, "God, I can't take any more," He is only saying one thing: "Cheer up; things are going to get worse!"

For this reason, we believers must develop the fruit of longsuffering, today, if we hope to "contend with horses" and survive "the swelling of Jordan" as circumstances worsen.

The second function of the fruit of longsuffering is to promote unity among believers. God's will for local bodies and for the Body of Christ as a whole is that the individual members be in unity in the Spirit and in faith:

> *And he gave some, apostles; and some, prophets; and some, evangelists; and some, pastors and teachers: For the perfecting of the saints, for the work of the ministry, for the edifying of the body of Christ: Till we all come in the unity of the faith, and of the knowledge of the Son of God, unto a perfect man, unto the measure of the stature of the fullness of Christ.*
>
> *Ephesians 4:11–13*

Unity among relationships in the family or local church will not be achieved until the individual members become like God by developing the fruit of longsuffering. Any group of people operating in longsuffering will bring glory to God:

Now the God of patience and consolation grant you to be like-minded one toward another according to Christ Jesus: That ye may with one mind and one mouth glorify God, even the Father of our Lord Jesus Christ.

Romans 15:5, 6

In the following parable, Jesus taught how the fruit of longsuffering enables believers to overlook the faults in one another:

Therefore is the kingdom of heaven likened unto a certain king, which would take account of his servants. And when he had begun to reckon, one was brought unto him, which owed him ten thousand talents. But for as much as he had not to pay, his lord commanded him to be sold, and his wife, and children, and all that he had, and payment to be made. The servant therefore fell down, and worshipped him, saying, "Lord, have patience with me, and I will pay thee all." Then the lord of that servant was moved with compassion, and loosed him, and forgave him the debt. But the same servant went out, and found one of his fellow servants, which owed him an hundred pence: and he laid hands on him, and took him by the throat, saying, "Pay me that thou owest." And his fellow servant fell down at his feet, and besought him, saying, "Have patience with me, and I will pay thee all." And he would not: but went and cast him into prison, till he should pay the debt.

Matthew 18:23–30

The debt-ridden servant appealed for his lord to be long-suffering when he cried: "Lord, have patience with me, and I will pay thee all" (v. 26). Therefore, it was because of his longsuffering, or patience, that the Lord of that servant was able to overlook the debt that was owed him, even though it was ten thousand talents (excess of nine million dollars). In the same respect, believers today can overlook and lovingly forgive the faults of one another only through the development of the fruit of longsuffering.

The reaction of the forgiven servant to the debt owed him by his fellow servant, however, is more prevalent among believers in local churches today. His fellow servant appealed to him to be longsuffering when "He fell down at his feel, and besought him, saying, Have patience with me, and I will pay thee all" (v. 29). Because the forgiven servant lacked longsuffering, he was not able to overlook and forgive, which would have enabled him to release his fellow servant from the bondage of the debt, a hundred pence (approximately fifteen dollars).

This is a type or symbol of what often occurs in local churches today. When fault meets no patience, the result is unforgiveness, bitterness, and strife; but when fault encounters longsuffering, there is forgiveness, mercy, and love. Thus, a group of believers who are striving to develop the fruit of longsuffering will overlook one another's faults, creating an atmosphere of love and unity in the local body.

Therefore, contrary to what most Christians think, their individual faults are not the reason for strife and division among them. Since there will always be unperfected believers, there will always be faults, until the Lord—the generous Forgiver—returns to establish His earthly kingdom in which there will be nothing but perfect peace and harmony. That peace and harmony will not exist because believers will have been made so perfect they will be incapable of error, but because Christ will be reigning and ruling in their hearts as well as over their lives.

If that is so, if peace and harmony do not depend upon the absence of fault but on the presence of Christ, then strife and divisions among believers must not be caused by their faults. Rather, they are the result of a lack of patience among the fellow servants.

> *Put on therefore, so the elect of God, holy and beloved, bowels of mercies, kindness, humbleness of mind, meekness, longsuffering; Forbearing one another, and forgiving one another, if any man has a quarrel against any: even as Christ forgave you, so also do ye.*
> *Colossians 3:12, 13*

Longsuffering prevents unforgiveness. According to Colossians 3:12, however, longsuffering must be "put on"; meaning that each believer is responsible for cultivating it in his life. The first sign of development after the process of cultivation has begun will be forbearance and forgiveness after the manner of Christ (v. 13).

> *Be patient therefore, brethren, unto the coming of*

the Lord. Behold, the husbandman waiteth for the precious fruit of the earth, and hath long patience for it, until he receive the early and latter rain. Be ye also patient; establish your hearts: for the coming of the Lord draweth nigh. Grudge not one against another, brethren, lest ye be condemned: behold, the judge standeth before the door.

James 5:7–9

In verses seven and eight of this passage, James is admonishing the Church to be patient, or longsuffering, because the coming of the Lord may be delayed. To many who have been watching and expecting His return, it seems that it indeed should have already taken place. James had one main concern for believers in case of such a delay. Of all the things he could have mentioned that might destroy the Church—such as Satan, evil spirits, strongholds—he chose this one to warn against: "Grudge not one against another...." (v. 9).

Since the word grudge means "to murmur or to complain," James is actually admonishing believers to be longsuffering with one another. Otherwise, they will destroy themselves as Paul warns in Galatians 5:15: "but if ye bite and devour one another, take heed that ye be not consumed one of another."

Many Christians, who should be running this race with endurance, so easily fall into the snare of the devil in that they bite and devour one another over insignificant things. For example, some actually consume one another because they feel slighted. They individually think and murmur such statements as: "He didn't sit by me at church like he usually does; I wonder what he's got against me." "I waved at her on the street yesterday and she didn't even look my way; she's ignoring me for some reason." "The minister didn't seek me out to shake my hand after the serve; he deliberately snubbed me!"

Then they proceed to feel sorry for themselves and complain and criticize, rather than seizing the opportunity to develop the fruit of longsuffering through overlooking a fault—whether that fault was real or only imagined.

God is raising up people who will be spiritually equipped to "run with the footmen," "contend with horses," and stand through the "swelling of the Jordan" (Jeremiah 12:5). Unfortunately, many believers today are barely keeping up with the turtles (much less horses) as they whine and cry over hurt feelings resulting from the alleged faults of others. What will these people do when the real afflictions, persecutions, and betrayals described in Luke 21:12, 16, 17 begin to come to pass? How will they be able to face possible imprisonment and death in that day if they can't even endure being slighted now?

Through the development of the fruit of longsuffering, God is preparing His people to be overcomers who will be able to endure the end-time persecutions that lie ahead. That preparation process begins today. The first step is simply to overlook the faults of the brethren.

Overcomers will forgive those who disagree and quarrel with them. They will work to keep strife out of the Church at all costs (short of producing strife themselves by their avoidance of it). This implies seeking harmony with their brethren, even though they may be right and their brother wrong. Faced with a dispute or a division with another believer, an overcomer will ask forgiveness, thus throwing cold water on the argument and extinguishing the fire of strife in the Church before it has an opportunity to spread.

This is longsuffering, *a quality that is sadly lacking and desperately need in the Church of Jesus Christ today.*

The third function of longsuffering is to enable believers to obtain the promises contained in the Word of God:

> *That ye be not slothful, but followers of them who through faith and patience inherit the promises. For when God made promises to Abraham, because he could swear by no greater, he swear by himself, Saying, Surely blessing I will bless thee, and multiplying I will multiply thee. And so, after he had patiently endured, he obtained the promise.*
>
> *Hebrews 6:12–15*

Abraham obtained the promise of a son only after patiently enduring. Since this time of patient endurance consisted of twenty-five years (Genesis 12:4; 17:17), Abraham obviously obtained the promise through the development of the fruit of longsuffering in his life. This is the principle contained in Hebrews 10:36, and it applies to believers today: "For ye have need of patience, that, after ye have done the will of God, ye might receive the promise."

In order to evaluate the need of patience in his life, a

believer should ask himself the following questions: "Are the promises in God's Word valid for today? Do they pertain to me and my life? Have I ever claimed a promise and nothing happened?" If we are totally honest, we will have to admit that to say "yes" to the first two questions, we must also honestly answer "yes" to the third one as well. We have all experienced those times when we have claimed a promise of God and yet never received the manifestation of it. The primary reason this happens is because we fail to exercise patience, or endurance.

Quite frankly, many times when the average Christian claims a promise, he prays just "to give God a shot at the problem." In the back of his mind, he is thinking, "I'll pray and believe for two weeks (or two months or two years); if the answer hasn't come by then, I'm going to go with Plan B." Except for the intervention of God, nine times out of ten anyone who prays like that will end up going with Plan B! It is only when a believer prays and is willing to stand forever, if necessary, to see the manifestation of the answer to his prayer that he will ever receive what he has asked. True faith, like true love, never gives up; "it beareath all things,...endureth all things" (1 Corinthians 13:7).

Finally, my brethren, be strong in the Lord, and in the power of his might. Put on the whole armour of God, that ye may be able to stand against the wiles of the devil. For we wrestle not against flesh and blood, but against principalities, against powers, against the rulers of the darkness of this world, against spiritual wickedness in high places. Wherefore take unto you the whole armour of God, that ye may be able to withstand in the evil day, and having done all, to stand. Stand therefore, having your loins girt about with truth, and having on the breastplate of righteousness.

Ephesians 6:10–14

The Word of God teaches that after we have done all we know to do, then we must stand. After we have built up our faith and fasted and prayed and put on the whole armor of God, we must recognize the necessity and the importance of standing. It is in the matter of standing, however, that most Christians fail. In this evil day, the fruit of longsuffering will enable us to stand and obtain the promises of God.

"Therefore I say unto you, What things soever ye desire, when ye pray, believe that ye receive them, and ye shall have them" (Mark 11:24). In this scripture our Lord promises: "...and ye shall have them." This places the entire responsibility of manifesting answers to prayers wholly upon God. So whether it takes a moment, a month, or a year for the answer to manifest makes no difference. Time is not a consideration in prayer. The answer will come in accordance to God's divine decree and plan. Praying is our part; timing is the Lord's. He knows the perfect solution to every prayer, and He also knows exactly when to manifest that solution for maximum benefit to all concerned.

The writer of Hebrews admonishes us: "Let us hold fast the profession of our faith without wavering:" (for he is faithful that promised) (Hebrews 10:23). God will be faithful to perform His Word. It is those who believe that Word and who are willing to stand on it until the answer manifests who will obtain the promises.

We believers should take comfort in the fact that everything we believe for in accordance with God's Word will be manifested. But we should also be aware of the fact that God will make us stand for it. Those who have developed the fruit of longsuffering will stand regardless of the length of time it takes. By so doing, they will be adding faith to that fruit of patience. According to Hebrews 6:12, that is exactly how the promises are obtained: "that ye be not slothful, but followers of them who through faith and patience inherit the promises."

God requires us believers to stand so He can see if we are just talking words, or if we are expressing faith. Abraham stood for twenty-five years (Genesis 12:4, 17:17), Caleb for forty-five years (Joshua 14:10), and Noah approximately one hundred years (Genesis 5:32; 7:6). The ability of these men to hold fast to God's promises and to stand was in direct proportion to the degree of development of the fruit of longsuffering in their individual lives.

This also is true of believers today who have claimed the promises of God for themselves. The promises of God are for all believers; they are claimed by those with faith—but they are *obtained* by those with patience.

The first way in which we believers may cultivate the fruit of longsuffering is by keeping the Word of the Lord. This principle was taught by Jesus in the parable of the sower and the seed in Luke 8:4–15. The sower sowed the seed, and some fell by the wayside, some fell upon a rock, and some fell among thorns. None of this seed produced fruit, simply because it was not capable of growing to maturation.

According to verse 8, however, that which fell on good ground "sprang up, and bare fruit a hundredfold." Jesus said very plainly in verse 11: "Now the parable is this: The seed is the word of God." He also explained what constituted the "good ground" in believers' hearts which is conducive to producing a hundredfold fruit: "But that on the good ground are they, which in an honest and good heart, having heard the word, keep it, and bring forth fruit with patience" (v. 15).

Believers often hear a teaching, and it is the very truth they need to apply to their lives. They are sincerely desirous of walking in its light. They receive the truth with gladness and rejoice at the realization of how to overcome whatever their obstacle is. They walk in this truth for perhaps two weeks, but suddenly it just vanishes—in spite of the encouragement and gladness that it elicited in their hearts when it was first received.

The reason for this failure is that those who hear the teaching do not "bring forth fruit with patience" (v. 15). As a result, that Word has no enduring, or longsuffering, effect in the individual life of the hearer.

We who hear the Word of God with a good and honest heart must learn to keep the Word; that is, we must learn to hold fast to the Word if it is to have any type of lasting effect upon our lives. Otherwise, we will be like those spoken of by Jesus in Mark 4:16, 17:

And these are they likewise which are sown on stony ground; who, when they have heard the word, immediately receive it with gladness; And have no root in themselves, and so endure but for a time: afterward, when affliction or persecution ariseth for the word's sake, immediately they are offended.

Many believers hear a teaching, and in their hearts they desire to walk in it, but the Word is unable to take root in their lives because they lack the fruit of longsuffering, which is necessary if that seed is to abide in their hearts long enough to grow to maturation and produce fruit. Therefore, those who put forth the effort to keep the Word that they hear will cultivate the fruit of longsuffering, which in turn will enable them to keep even more of the Word.

In the Old Testament, God told Adam to "keep" the garden: "And the Lord God took the man, and put him into the Garden of Eden to dress it and to keep it" (Genesis 2:15). This work for *keep* in the Hebrew has the same meaning as the word used for *keep* in the Greek in Luke 8:15 when Jesus admonished His followers to "keep" (the Word), "and bring forth fruit with patience."

Because Adam did not fulfill his God-given responsibility of keeping the Garden of Eden, he had to live on a lower level than God ever intended for his life. The same is true of believers today who do not keep the Word the Lord entrust to them—they find themselves living on a lower spiritual plain than their heavenly Father even intended for them to live on. Therefore, the reason there are so many spiritual "wrecks" in the Church today is not because Christians necessarily lack the opportunity to hear the Word; it is because they are not keeping the Word they do hear.

The numerous blessings associated with hearing the Word of God are always accompanied with the God-given responsibility of keeping that Word. Those whom God sees fulfilling their responsibilities will be granted to live on a much higher level, for He will trust them with the "keeping" of His "Eden"—that place where He is growing the spiritual tree of life (Genesis 2:9).

Know ye not, that to whom ye yield yourselves servants to obey, his servants ye are to whom ye obey; whether of sin unto death, or of obedience unto righteousness? But God be thanked, that ye were the servants of sin, but ye have obeyed from the heart that from of doctrine which was delivered you. Being then made free from sin, ye became the servants of righteousness.

Romans 6:16–18

The key to keeping the Word is to obey it from the heart. When believers obey the Word from their hearts, then they become the servants of righteousness. On the other hand, those who only have the Word in their heads are still likely to yield to temptations and be servants of sin. Therefore, it is only as the teaching of how to overcome those besetting sins extends from their heads to their hearts that they will obey it and will be set free from serving sin.

A price must be paid if we believers are to retain and obey the Word. First, we must reject the traditional thinking of going to meetings only for the purpose of rating a sermon. After any church service, believers will often be heard making such comments as: "Well, that was a good sermon" (often with the implication of "I got a goose-bump"); or, "Well, that sermon was pretty bad" (usually meaning, "I didn't like it because it made me uncomfortable").

We believers should always take seriously the teachings we hear—as long as those teachings line up with the revealed Word of God. When we are exposed to a truly acceptable biblical teaching, we should take the attitude that God Himself had us at that particular place at that particular time to hear that particular message.

Secondly, we must study the Word of God for ourselves. By so doing, we will keep the Word and obey it from our hearts and become the servants of righteousness.

God is not desirous that His children come under condemnation and fall into sin because they are not able of themselves to obey all the Word they hear. Instead, He desires for them to get the Word in their hearts, because then they will be set free from struggle and sin for the Word will do the work from within. According to Romans 6:17, those who get the Word in their hearts will be obedient to that Word. They will experience the fullness of the liberty that God intends for their lives.

In Hebrews 10:32 we read that the illumination of the Word of God produces endurance: "But call to remembrance the former days, in which, after ye were illuminated, ye endured a great fight of afflictions." It is after we are illuminated that we are capable of enduring even a vast opposition of afflictions. Thus, when a teaching is enlightened to our hearts, it will cultivate and develop within us the fruit of longsuffering.

The second way in which we believers may cultivate the fruit of longsuffering is by experiencing tribulation: "And not only so, but we glory in tribulations also: knowing that tribulation worketh patience" (Romans 5:3). The tribulations, or trials, that we believers experience "worketh" (achieve, produce) patience. Knowing that the fruit of longsuffering is being developed in our lives is the thing that makes us able to glory even in the midst of our trials.

The development of the fruit of longsuffering is truly something to be joyful about: "My brethren, count it all joy when ye fall into divers temptations; Knowing this, that the trying of your faith worketh patience" (James 1:2, 3). It is only through the recognizing of the importance of this particular fruit of the Spirit that we believers can obey the command to count it all joy.

It is not just the experiencing of trials, however, that produces longsuffering. If this were true, then every believer would have the fruit of longsuffering developed one- hundredfold in his life, for everyone experiences trials. Whether or not we believers benefit from our trials through developing patience is totally dependent upon our response to those trials. The degree of benefit from a trial is dependent upon one thing: the attitude we display during that trial. In times of tribulation, the question we must ask ourselves is: "While this is taking place, am I *waiting,* or am I *worrying?*"

Those who wait on God during their trials develop patience; whereas, those who worry through their tribulation only develop spiritual paralysis. "He giveth power to the faint; and to them that have no might he increaseth strength. Even the youths shall faint and be weary, and the young men shall utterly fall" (Isaiah 40:29, 30). This is a vivid description of many believers today who are going through trials; they are faint, weary, fallen. They are experiencing spiritual paralysis because of weariness. As a result, they are about to faint. The following verse, however, is a beautiful definition of longsuffering: "But they that wait upon the Lord shall renew their strength; they shall mount up with wings as eagles; they shall run, and not be weary; and they shall walk, and not faint" (Isaiah 40:31). The strength of believers who are patiently waiting upon the Lord during their trials will be evident as they rise about their circumstances, run without growing weary, and walk without fainting. The key to possessing this strength is to learn how to wait upon the Lord.

In Acts 1:4, Jesus commanded His disciples to "wait for the promise of the Father..." Their response to this command is a good example of how believers should wait upon God. They didn't gather in the upper room and begin to say to one another: "When is this thing ever going to manifest? We've been waiting here for so long now, and still nothing has happened." On the contrary, while they were waiting, "they all continue with one accord in prayer and supplication..." (Acts 1:14).

In times of trial, waiting on God means standing in earnest expectation and praying with supplications, intercessions, and thanksgiving. Believers who are truly waiting on God are eagerly anticipating the manifestation of the answer to their prayers.

The third way to develop the fruit of longsuffering is by maintaining hope:

> For we are saved by hope: but hope that is seen is not hope: for what a man seeth, why doth he yet hope for? But if we hope for that we see not, then do we with patience wait for it.
>
> Romans 8:24, 25

According to 1 Peter 1:13, hope produces a long-suffering heart: "Wherefore gird up the loins of your mind, be sober, and hope to the end for the grace that is to be brought unto you at the revelation of Jesus Christ." Believers who lose their hope will give up their patience. Actually, those who lose their hope lose their hearts: "Hope deferred maketh the heart sick: but when the desire cometh, it is a tree of life" (Proverbs 13:12). Believers should therefore cherish, nourish, and guard hope in their hearts, for it is an important contribution to the manifestation of the of their hearts' desires.

A believer must first maintain hope for himself if he is ever to be longsuffering. So often a Christian will make comments such as: "I can't make it." "There is absolutely no way that I can be an overcomer." "I just simply cannot endure to the end." Remarks such as these indicate that this particular person needs to develop hope for himself. They are also an indication of a possible lack of longsuffering in his life. A person with hope will patiently wait for God to move on his behalf; whereas one who has lost hope for himself will not be longsuffering toward God's work in his life.

Secondly, a believer must maintain hope during a time of trial. As long as he can see a mere speck of light at the end of the long, dark tunnel of his trial, there is hope. If the enemy, however, can steal that little ray of hope, then he will give up.

For example, if a person can no longer "see" his spouse saved, he will give up praying and believing for that salvation. In the same way, if a believer can no longer "see" the manifestation of his healing, or the restoration of a broken relationship, or the victory over a besetting sin, he will give up and accept defeat in that area of his life. Any Christian who loses hope during his trial will eventually give up and no longer wait upon God. Thus, hope is vital in order to experience the manifestation of divine deliverance.

Thirdly, a believer must maintain hope in others. If he loses hope in someone, then he will become very bitter and short-tempered with that individual and will eventually experience unforgiveness toward him or her. He will also make statements such as: "He'll never make it." "There's just no hope for her." This happens frequently in marriages, churches, or in any other institution in which people who spend a lot of time together have the opportunity of really getting to know one another well.

Once again, a person who loses hope for others is like the servant in the parable of Jesus who would not overlook his fellow servant's fault because he lacked patience (Matthew 18:28–30). Loss of hope for someone always opens the door to strife in a relationship. Therefore, hope for the brethren is necessary if we believers are ever to be longsuffering toward one another.

Using Abraham as an example, the Word shows us how to maintain hope in these three areas:

> *Who against hope believed in hope, that he might become the father of many nations, according to that which was spoken, so shall thy seed be. And being not weak in faith, he considered not his own body now dead, when he was about a hundred years old, neither yet the deadness of Sarah's womb.*
>
> *Romans 4:18, 19*

God promised Abraham a son. In the natural, this looked hopeless. Abraham, however, did not view the situation through the natural. He viewed it through what God said concerning it. Only the Word of God can paint hope where there is no hope. We should always view adverse situations in our lives—whether they relate to our selves, our trials, or other people—through what God's Word says concerning those situations.

If the enemy can prevent us from finding out what the Word says concerning our trials, or if he can get us, who have been enlightened, to take our eyes off of what the Word of God says and onto what we think or feel, then we will lose hope and give up.

When we are experiencing physical distress, we will lose hope and give up if we lose sight of "by whose stripes ye were healed" (1 Peter 2:24). In the midst of financial distress, we will lose hope if we get our eyes off of what the Word of God says about our situation and thereby listen more to our fears than we do to our Father. When going through more difficult family situations, we will lose hope and give up if we lose sight of the promises of God and listen instead to the doubts of the enemy. Those who lose hope will not patiently wait for the manifestation of the promise.

> *And we desire that every one of you do shew the same diligence to the full assurance of hope unto the end: That ye be not slothful, but followers of them who through faith and patience inherit the promises.*
>
> *Hebrews 6:11, 12*

During difficult and seemingly hopeless times, our top priority should be to find out what the Word of God declares to be true about our situation: but if we hope for that we see not, then do we with patience wait for it (Romans 8:25). Hope, patience, and receiving the promises blend beautifully together, for hope produces patience, which is the preservative for faith in the fragile human heart.

Every man surely is aware of the brevity of life; who honestly desires to spend his precious time suffering? The child of God, however, who yields his life in humble trust and obedience to his loving Father, will say with David of old: "My times are in thy hand..." (Psalm 31:15). He will learn to say it both during his times of pleasure and his times of suffering.

Blessed is the person who develops the fruit of long-suffering, for he will discover in his life that truly "...all things work together for good to them that love God, to them who are the called according to his purpose" (Romans 8:28).

The fruit of longsuffering is indeed a "benefit...of our salvation" (Psalm 68:19), for it enables us to live more meaningful lives by helping us to profit from our times of suffering, so that none of our days be lost.

OPENING THE DOOR
TO GOOD WORKS

"But the fruit of the Spirit is...gentleness, goodness..."

Galatians 5:22

The fruit of gentleness may be appropriately defined as the fruit of kindness. According to W.E. Vine, one Greek scholar described gentleness, or kindness, as "a kindly disposition toward others," whereas goodness is defined as "a kindly activity on their behalf."

In other words, gentleness is what people see in a believer and goodness is what they outwardly experience from that believer. If a Christian, therefore, does not have a kind disposition toward people, then he cannot possibly manifest goodness toward them. Since these two fruits are so closely intertwined, they must be considered and studied together.

Without kindness, there will be no manifested goodness. This is especially true in the case of forgiveness: "And be ye kind to one another, tenderhearted, forgiving one another, even as God for Christ's sake hath forgiven you" (Ephesians 4:32). Kindness brings a tender disposition, which is especially necessary in manifesting the good works of forgiveness.

Jesus Himself spoke of these two fruits, but He called them by different names:

> *Ye are the salt of the earth: but if the salt have lost his savour, wherewith shall it be salted? it is thenceforth good for nothing, but to be cast out, and to be trodden under foot of men. Ye are the light of the world. A city that is set on a hill cannot be hid. Neither do men light a candle, and put it under a bushel, but on a candlestick; and it giveth light unto all that are in the house. Let your light so shine before men, that they may see your good works, and glorify your Father which is in heaven.*
>
> *Matthew 5:13–16*

Salt is a type of the fruit of kindness, for it brings seasoning to the earth. Anyone who has to deal with the public is painfully aware of how rare it is to find a kind person in the world today. Many people in our society are so rude and overbearing that encountering a truly kind person is like finding an oasis in the desert. Therefore, typical of salt, a believer's kindness brings savor, or seasoning, to the earth.

Light is a type of the fruit of goodness. In Matthew 5:16 Jesus said that light is a person's good works, or works of goodness. He taught His followers: Let your light so shine before men, that they may see your good works...Since goodness is defined as a kindly activity on behalf of others, then kindness within must always precede outward acts of goodness. When a believer's salt, or kindness, is savory towards another, then his light will automatically shine through the manifestation of his good works.

The ministry of the Apostle Paul to the Thessalonians is an example of how kindness must precede goodness:

> *But we were gentle among you, even as a nurse cherisheth her children: So being affectionately desirous of you, we were willing to have imparted unto you, not the gospel of God only, but also our own souls, because ye were dear unto us. For ye remember, brethren, our labour and travail: for labouring night and day, because we would not be chargeable unto any of you, we preached unto you the gospel of God.*
>
> 1 *Thessalonians* 2:7–9

The gentleness, or kindness, mentioned in verse 7 opened the door to the good works referred to in verse 9. *Kindness is the only door out of which goodness can flow.*

Paul recognized the precedence of kindness and demonstrated how this principle operates in the relationship of a mother and her children (1 Thessalonians 2:7, 8). Since a mother's heart is very tender and gentle (kind) toward her children, works of goodness manifest through her on their behalf.

Jesus also taught that kindness must precede goodness: Ye are the salt of the earth: but if the salt have lost his savour, wherewith shall it be salted? It is thenceforth good for nothing, but to be cast out, and trodden under foot of men (Matthew 5:13). Believers are the salt of the earth, but when they lose their savor, of kindness, Jesus said that they are "good for nothing."

This statement of Jesus coincides with the meaning of the Greek word translated gentleness in Galatians 5:22, where the fruits of the Spirit are listed. This word is *chrestotes* (*kray-stot'-ace*), meaning "usefulness."

A believer who loses his kindly disposition toward someone automatically loses his usefulness for God. Jesus said that when this happens, such a person might as well be cast out and trodden under foot of men (Matthew 5:13). Therefore, the degree to which we believers are useful to God is determined by the degree to which the fruit of kindness has developed in our lives, for believers are only as good (useful) to God as they are good (kind) to people.

> *Do all things without murmurings and disputings: That ye may be blameless and harmless, the sons of God, without rebuke, in the midst of a crooked and perverse nation, among whom ye shine as lights in the world.*
>
> *Philippians 2: 14, 15*

According to Paul, if believers murmur, dispute, and complain, their lights will not shine. The murmurings and disputings cause their dispositions to change, causing their lights to cease shining; that is, it causes their good works to cease being manifested. The fruit of kindness must be developed in our lives if we are to "shine as lights in the world" (v. 15).

If the enemy can steal or distort the fruit of kindness in a believer's life, then the fruit of goodness will automatically wither. Jesus said we believers are first the salt of the earth, then the light of the world. So, if the enemy can take away our savor, our light will not shine. For this reason, this study will deal specifically and exclusively with the function and the development of the fruit of kindness, or gentleness.

The main function of the fruit of kindness is that it enables believers to be the salt of the earth. More specifically, being the salt of the earth performs three works. These three spiritual effects of kindness may be compared to three of the many physical attributes of salt.

The first function of the fruit of kindness is comparable to the purifying quality of salt upon the earth. Salt can be used as a fertilizer to prepare soil for bearing fruit. In the same way, kindness prepares the hearts of unbelievers for receiving the implantation of the seed of reconciliation:

> For we ourselves also were sometimes foolish, disobedient, deceived, serving divers lusts and pleasures, living in malice and envy, hateful, and hating one another. But after that the kindness and love of God our Savior toward man appeared, Not by works of righteousness which we have done, but according to his mercy he saved us, by the washing of regeneration, and renewing of the Holy Ghost.
>
> *Titus 3:3–5*

The majority of those who experience the New Birth do so because they first experience the loving kindness of

God, for kindness is a forerunner of regeneration. When an unbeliever experiences God's kindness, the soil of his heart is prepared to receive the seed of the Word. Then, as he hears the Word of regeneration, his receptive heart accepts that seed, which produces the fruit of reconciliation.

Believers, who are the salt of the earth, are God's expression of His kindness and goodness to the world. The fruit of kindness in the lives of His children is the fullness of Jesus manifested to the world.

> *Likewise, ye wives, be in subjection to your own husbands; that, if any obey not the word, they also may without the word be won by the conversation of the wives; While they behold your chaste conversation coupled with fear. Whose adorning let it not be that outward adorning of plaiting the hair, and of wearing of gold, or of putting on of apparel; But let it be the hidden man of the heart, in that which is not corruptible, even the ornament of a meek and quiet spirit, which is in the sight of God of great price.*
>
> 1 *Peter* 3:1–4

The word conversation in verses 1 and 2 actually means "*behavior.*" In other words, believers can reach a place in their lives where, not only through hearing the word of God people are saved, but unbelievers will be won to the Lord simply by watching the lives of believers and beholding their "chaste" (Greek word hagnos, "immaculate") manner of life.

Not only will they observe the holy lives of believers, but also their kind dispositions; that is, the "meek and quiet spirit" of their "hidden man of the heart" (v. 4). In this way, unbelievers can be won without the Word (v. 1). This principle not only applies to husbands and wives, but to any relationship between believers and unbelievers.

Quite often, unbelievers will notice a difference in a particular believer's manner of life in that he does not publicly practice any bad habits such as cursing, smoking, or drinking. They take note that he is very self-disciplined in prayer, Bible study, and church attendance. Yet, they still do not become converted. One reason for this may be that this particular believer does not have a meek and quiet spirit; his light may be hidden under the "bushel" of a rude disposition. Therefore, believers who are frustrated because no one seems to be interested in receiving their Christian witness should check the degree of development of the fruit of kindness in their lives.

How can we believers be rude to people, and then expect a favorable response when we try to witness to them? It seems absurd that anyone would even try to win others to his way of life when he himself is so obnoxious and unattractive. Yet this very thing occurs frequently.

For example, a wife may stay at home, read her Bible, and pray while her unbelieving husband is out on the town drinking and carousing, but if she become angry and upset with him when he comes home, then he will either ignore or scorn the Bible in her lap and the prayer on her lips. However, if that wife develops a meek and quiet spirit and greets her wayward husband at the door with the loving kindness of God, then she will get his attention. He will notice her chaste manner of living. The fruit of kindness will fertilize his heart so that he will receive the Word that is working in her, and thus be won to the Lord. He will not be won by an emotional sermon or a Gospel tract or a doctrinal dissertation. Instead, he will be won by the living epistle being enacted before his eyes by his wife, a visual representation of the loving kindness of the heavenly Father.

Rude treatment of those in public service is another example of how we believers often present a negative witness to others of what it means to be a Christian, a "little Christ."

Suppose a particular waitress overhears the people at her assigned table talking. They seem so happy and carefree, so genuinely excited about this person they are discussing, she asks herself, "Whom are they talking about?" She listens more closely and this time she decides, "Oh, these people are talking about Jesus. I wonder if they know Him personally." So, she makes a mental note that for the next hour she will keep in close contact with these folks who claim to be representatives of the Living Lord.

She notices a closeness and a love between them so she asks herself, "Is this the way Jesus-people treat each other? That's wonderful." She also notices, however, that as she approaches the table to take their orders they refuse to make eye contact with her. Then as they give her their individual orders, they are self-centered and flippant in their attitude, seeming to care nothing for the difficulty they are causing her by their lack of order and sensitivity. She can only assume that this is the way Jesus Himself must act.

Later, when she returns with their food, she catches part of their conversation: "Church sure was good today." The Lord has really been blessing *me* lately." "Oh, hallelujah, God is so good."

She thinks how lonely and how frustrated she has been lately, having to deal with the problems in her life all alone. Yet these people seem to pay no attention to her at all as they proudly and piously "praise the Lord" for all *their* blessings before hurriedly digging in to enjoy *their* meal. Again she assumes that this selfishness and indifference is also Jesus' attitude.

She is still wondering about some of the remarks she overheard these people make, when she suddenly realized one of them is speaking to her in a very patronizing and condescending manner. "Oh, I'm sorry, sir," she replies in haste, "my mistake. Did you want something?" Noting his sharply worded request, she hurries off to the kitchen to fill his order. As she does, she thinks to herself, "So this is what Jesus Christ is like."

As she pours their after-dinner coffee, she notices how freely they laugh and joke among themselves, but she can't help but notice also their seeming unwillingness to share the source of that laughter and joy with her.

As they get up to go, in their preoccupation with their own interests and concerns, they do not even acknowledge her presence, much less the service she has rendered them. While busily cleaning up the mess they left on the table, she discovers that one of them has left a tract entitled "The Four Spiritual Laws." The tract is weighed down with a bright, shiny new quarter—her tip.

Silently passing off the whole experience with a shrug of the shoulder, she drops the quarter into her apron pocket and the tract into the nearest trashcan. The affair is quickly wiped from her memory, just as she wipes away from the tablecloth the crumbs left behind by these "representatives" of the Son of God. The incident is soon forgotten, but unfortunately the impression remains for a long, long time.

Jesus pleads with His followers to be good representatives of Him. He reminds them: "Ye are the salt of the earth: but if the salt have lost his savour, wherewith shall it be salted?" (Matthew 5:13).

The second function of the fruit of kindness is comparable to the universal quality of salt. From the most elite restaurant in a huge metropolitan complex to the humblest village café, salt is universally identical. It tastes the same no matter where one shakes it. Just as salt is "no respecter of restaurants," the fruit of kindness is no respecter of persons; regardless of how unsavory a person or a situation might be, it always has the same quality and always produces the same flavor.

"But if ye have respect to persons, ye commit sin, and are convinced of the law as transgressors" (James 2:9). Being respecters of persons is one of the most widespread sins in the Body of Christ today. Yet believers do not realize that they are *sinners* committing sins and thus in need of forgiveness when they allow themselves to have respect of persons.

Many Christians exhibit the attitude that not everyone is privileged enough to experience their savor. They are like salt and pepper—a little salt here, a little pepper there—a little kindness here, a little judgment there. This is sin, and the reason it exists within the Body of Christ is because the fruit of kindness has not been developed in the individual lives of believers.

Since the fruit of kindness enables believers to always be the same, regardless of where they are or who they are with, it also enables them to be at peace with everyone. Of course, there will always be those who oppose, but that doesn't bother the "salty" believer; he can be at peace in any situation.

The first area in which we believers need to remain "salty" is with unbelievers. Knowing that there is a truth in the Word concerning our being separate from evil-doers, many Christians go to such an extreme to separate themselves from sin that they become unkind to sinners. Separation from the world, however, does not imply being rude to those who are in the world. How can the people of the earth be salted if the salt loses its savor every time they come in contact with it? In other words, how can we believers expect to fertilize the hearts of sinners if we are not kind to them?

To illustrate, let's take the example of that group of believers who went into the restaurant to order a meal. This time, let's imagine that they are sensitive to the needs of others about them, but that the waitress is surly and rude as she comes to serve them. Suddenly, however, she overhears them talking about Jesus, and her whole disposition is transformed right before their eyes. She boldly approaches them, smiles sweetly with a knowing look, and says, "Excuse me. Are you talking about Jesus?"

Those at the table are startled at the abrupt change, but dare not ask, "What happened? Aren't you that rude woman who was waiting on us a few minutes ago?"

Proudly she continues, "I just knew you were Christians; I am too. I go down to 'First Church' myself."

What happened? Her disposition and manner toward these people changed when she realized they were Christians.

Many people are like this waitress in that they are rude around unbelievers, but can turn the kindness on and off to accommodate those whom they suspect of being Christians. That is not the way we believers should act. We should be as kind to unbelievers as we are to the members of our own church body.

God desires that the fruit of kindness so permeate a local body of believers that anyone He might send their way can walk through the door, be saved, filled with His Holy Spirit, and ministered to out of hearts abounding in the love and compassion of God Himself. The Father desires to trust His children to the point that He can enlarge their spiritual family by sending anyone, regardless of his station in life, into their fellowship and know that he will not be treated according to what he can or cannot do for the benefit of either the individual member or of the church as a whole. In other words, God desires that the fruit of kindness be cultivated and developed among His people to a greater degree than ever before, because today "the harvest truly is plenteous" (Matthew 9:37)—and the time of harvest is come.

The second area in which we believers need to remain "salty" is in our families, especially with our spouse and children. Many believers have no trouble whatsoever being kind to people—until they get home, and then "threshold metamorphosis" sets in. The moment their foot steps across the threshold of their home, they change from a kind, loving person into thoughtless, rude ogre.

For example, families are often in the process of arguing and wounding one another with cruel, hateful words when suddenly the phone rings. One of the family members picks up the receiver and sweetly answers, "Hello? Why yes, he's here. One moment, please." Then he covers up the mouthpiece of the receiver, and rudely yells, "Hey, come answer this thing—it's for you!"

Actions such as these are an indication of a lack of kindness. Believers must realize that when they treat their own spouse or children with less respect and courtesy than they treat others, they are committing sin.

That fruit of kindness enables one to be gentle and sweet to the members of his family, in spite of all the little irritations that go with living together. This fruit is needful in light of the fact that, regardless of what the popular song says, someone does know what goes on "behind closed doors." That someone is God. Our heavenly Father knows exactly what takes place in the individual households of His children, and He deals with them accordingly.

God is very much concerned with how we believers treat our spouse and children. In fact, He is so concerned that He impressed upon the Apostle Paul to write: "But if any provide not for his own, and specially for those of his own house, he hath denied the faith, and is worse than an infidel" (1 Timothy 5:8). This issue of family kindness was so important to Paul that he dealt with it in at least two other letters:

> *So ought men to love their wives as their own bodies. He that loveth his wife loveth himself. For no man ever yet hated his own flesh; but nourisheth and cherisheth it, even as the Lord the church. (Ephesians 5:28, 29) That they may teach the young women to be sober, to love their husbands, to love their children, To be discreet, chaste, keepers at home, good, obedient to their own husbands, that the word of God be not blasphemed.*
>
> *Titus 2:4, 5*

The fruit of kindness enables husbands to be kind to their wives no matter how they respond; and the fruit of kindness also enables wives to be kind to their husbands regardless of how they act. The fruit of kindness, therefore, enables husbands and wives to fulfill the Word concerning how they are to treat one another.

The third function of the fruit of kindness is comparable to the antiseptic quality of salt. Like salt, the fruit of kindness has antiseptic qualities that make it useful as a mouthwash. As the fruit is developed in the heart of a believer and manifested in his mouth, it will clean up his words. It will enable him to fulfill Ephesians 4:29: "Let no corrupt communication proceed out of your mouth, but that which is good to the use of edifying, that it may minister grace unto the hearers."

A believer can come to a place in his life in which he speaks absolutely no words of corruption but only words of grace and edification. However, this is possible only when his speech is seasoned with salt, or kindness: "Let your speech be always with grace, seasoned with salt, that ye may know how ye ought to answer every man" (Colossians 4:6). When a believer's tongue is seasoned with kindness, it will affect the words he speaks. So many Christians are flippant and frivolous with their tongues because the fruit of kindness has not been developed in their lives.

The first effect that the fruit of kindness will have upon a believer's mouth is that it will enable him to turn away wrath: "A soft answer turneth away wrath: but grievous words stir up anger" (Proverbs 15:1). There have been countless times in each of our lives when a kind response would have prevented a misunderstanding, argument, and fight containing many, many grievous words. All that division, all that strife, all that bitterness, and all that contention could have been avoided if only our tongue had been seasoned with the fruit of kindness.

The second effect that the fruit of kindness will have upon a believer's mouth is that it will enable him to withhold wounds: "The words of a talebearer are as wounds, and they go down into the innermost parts of the belly" (Proverbs 18:8). A talebearer is one who speaks "whisperings", that is, one who is unkind in his words.

Unkind words are very hurtful to people, leaving deep, festering wounds in their hearts. It is probably less painful for most people for someone to slap them in the face than it is for that same person to say hurtful things to or about them. Since a slap is physical, in time the physical pain it produces will go away; but slanderous words are not so quickly forgotten or overcome because they cut right through to the innermost parts of a person's being.

Words possess a power to wound the heart like nothing else can: "Death and life are in the power of the tongue: and they that love it shall eat the fruit thereof" (Proverbs 18:21). This truth is very obvious in the area of foolish jesting. Most people who laugh with those who make jokes about them think later, "I know he was only joking, but did he really mean what he said about me?" For this reason, we believers should always be careful to watch what we say in jest, to whom we say it, when we say it, and especially why we say it.

"Pleasant words are as a honeycomb, sweet to the soul, and health to the bones" (Proverbs 16:24). Believers whose speech has been salted with the fruit of kindness will be able to speak pleasant words that bring health rather than harmful words that wound, for "life" as well as "death" in the power of the tongue (Proverbs 18:21). Anybody can speak pleasant words when things are going well, but believers who have developed the fruit of kindness can speak pleasant words even in the midst of trials and persecutions. This is just another attribute of salt: the power to promote healing.

The third effect that the fruit of kindness will have upon a believer's mouth is to enable him to cease strife: "Where no wood is, there the fire goeth out: so where there is no talebearer, the strife ceaseth" (Proverbs 26:20). Strife within a local church will continue to spread until it encounters a believer who has the fruit of kindness in his life. The devil needs only one talebearer to ignite a rumor, and the resulting slander and gossip will spread among believers until it encounters and is extinguished by a heart full of kindness. When strife enters the truly kind heart, it will be quenched before it has the opportunity to spread by issuing from the mouth: "...where there is no talebearer, the strife ceaseth" (Proverbs 26:20).

Jesus said: "Neither do men light a candle, and put it under a bushel, but on a candlestick; and it giveth light unto all that are in the house" (Matthew 5:15). According to Proverbs 20:27, the candle which Jesus is speaking of is the spirit of man: "The spirit of man is the candle of the Lord searching all the inward parts of the belly." Those who have been born of the Spirit of God have their candles lit; they already have the potential within them of being kind. As a matter of fact, when most people are born again, they experience such an overwhelming sense of kindness that they are "overly" kind. They have a tendency to want to give away practically everything they own and do things constantly for others. Their brothers in the Lord are almost tempted to put a restrain on them, for after all, too much fertilizer can kill the soil.

Jesus wants the candles that He has lit to be placed on candlesticks so that light might shine to all that are in the house. Why? So they may see our good works and glorify our Father which is in heaven (Matthew 5:15, 16). Jesus wants our light to shine so that everyone may see the kindness and the goodness of God. Jesus desires this because it glorifies the Father, which is why we should desire it as well.

In Matthew 5:15, however, Jesus warned those whose candles were lit to guard against bushels that would prevent their lights from shining. *Bushels* are anything that would come against a believer and distort his disposition in order to affect his kindness, which inevitably quenches his goodness.

There are many "bushel-heads" in the Body of Christ today. They began the Christian walk with kindness, but after a period of time that flame within them grew dimmer and dimmer, until finally it flickered and disappeared. Like the church of Ephesus in Revelation 2:4, 5, such people have left their first love. Within them is a very beautiful candle that has been lit by the flame of God's loving kindness, but their light has been quenched by the bushel of a distorted disposition.

Therefore, the fruit of kindness does not necessarily need to be cultivated in order for it to be developed, at least not in the same sense that the other fruits of the Spirit do. Instead, we believers must concentrate on keeping the bushels off of our dispositions so the fruit of kindness may develop in our individual lives, producing thirty, sixty, and one hundredfold.

The first major bushel in the Body of Christ today is offense. As soon as a believer gets offended, his disposition changes instantly: "A brother offended is harder to be won than a strong city: and their contentions are like the bars of a castle" (Proverbs 18:19). An offended believer displays contention, not kindness. Regardless of who has offended him—whether it was the minister, a fellow believer, or someone outside his local church—bars rise, and he instantly exhibits a contentious disposition to those about him.

> *Then shall they deliver you up to be afflicted, and shall kill you: and ye shall be hated of all nations for my name's sake. And then shall many be offended, and shall betray one another, and shall hate one another.*
> *Matthew 24:9–10*

According to Jesus, two consequences of becoming offended are hatred and betrayal. Jesus is not referring here to unbelievers, either. He is speaking of those believers whose dispositions change as a result of being offended. To betray means "to turn against what was once followed." This is happening in the churches today, and it is a very serious problem. Many believers who have been enjoying the praise, the worship, the teaching, and the presence of God in the place where the Lord has set them, have suddenly gotten their feelings hurt and have turned against what they once embraced. As soon as they became offended, they changed. Now they are "Harder to be won than a strong city" (Proverbs 18:19).

A minister who speaks the Word of God boldly will have the unfortunate experience of offending people from time to time for the Word's sake. Any minister who has gone through this experience can testify that the first thing he notices in these instances is that the offended party is no longer kind toward him. The person may still fellowship and worship with him, but the minister can sense that the kindness which once flowed from heart to heart now has a bushel on it.

Generally, most people know when someone is faking kindness and when it is truly flowing from the depths of the heart. An offended believer is like "the bars of a castle" (Proverbs 18:19). All he needs is an ounce of encouragement, and he will talk about, and thereby imprison, that minister whom he holds responsible for offending him.

When we believers are tempted to get offended, we must stop pointing at either the real or the imagined faults of others and start checking ourselves. If our dispositions have changed, we have a problem, for if we allow ourselves to change, then our kindness will be quenched.

It is the duty of every believer to avoid offense—taking it, as well as giving it!

The first way to overcome taking offense is through the Word of God. Jesus said: "These things have I spoken unto you, that ye should not be offended" (John 16:1). Jesus meant this literally. It is a spiritual principle that believers who are diligent about studying the Word will become much less likely to get their feelings hurt. This truth is also expressed in the Old Testament: "Great peace have they which love thy law: and nothing shall offend them" (Psalm 119:165). The only reason a believer ever gets offended is because he is shallow in God's Word:

> *And these are they likewise which are sown on stony ground; who, when they have heard the word, immediately receive it with gladness; And have no root in themselves, and so endure but for a time: afterward, when affliction or persecution ariseth for the word's sake, immediately they are offended.*
>
> *Mark 4:16, 17*

There are those within the Church who are not individually rooted in the Word. Therefore, they become offended when encountered with affliction or persecution for the Word's sake. Sometimes they become offended at the mere teaching and preaching of the Word.

Many ministers are aware of this situation and can detect when their sermons become offensive to different ones in the congregation. This is especially true in smaller fellowships. Often the minister of a small church knows who will have the opportunity to be offended even before he delivers his sermon.

This is why many ministers encounter turmoil within and problems without that manifest themselves in some aspect of their ministry. They know what God is speaking to their heart to minister to the people, but they will not say it because they also know who it will offend. They especially hesitate if the person who might be offended is a big tither, for some ministers certainly do not want to risk offending a tither!

The problem lies with the person who gets offended when he hears the truth. This is why the Word of God states that in the last days people will not want to hear the truth and will seek out teachers who will tell them only what they want to hear:

> *For the time will come when they will not endure sound doctrine; but after their own lusts shall they heap to themselves teachers, having itching ears; And they shall turn away their ears from the truth, and shall be turned unto fables.*
>
> 2 *Timothy* 4:3, 4

Believers with a good and honest heart will refuse to be offended by the truth. As a result, they will become rooted and grounded in the Word of God and will not be offended at the affliction and persecution which will arise against them in these last days for the Word's sake.

On the other hand, those who do not get the Word in their hearts now will easily become offended and fall away. They will one day find themselves betraying the body that once ministered to them and helped them. They may even find themselves hating those very people whom they once loved the most. No believer should consider himself immune from the warning of our Lord in Matthew 24:10 but should begin taking the necessary precaution of getting the Word firmly established in his heart now.

The second way to overcome being offended is through the love of God:

> *Charity suffereth long, and is kind; charity envieth not; charity vaunteth not itself, is not puffed up, Doth not behave itself unseemly, seeketh not her own, is not easily provoked, thinketh no evil; Rejoiceth not in iniquity, but rejoiceth in the truth; Beareth all things, believeth all things, hopeth all things, endureth all things.*
>
> 1 *Corinthians* 13:4–7

Love is longsuffering (v. 4). Love is not easily provoked (v. 5). Love bears and endures all things (v. 7). In other words, love is not easily offended.

> *But ye, beloved, building up yourselves on your most holy faith, praying in the Holy Ghost, Keep yourselves in the love of God, looking for the mercy of our Lord Jesus Christ unto eternal life.*
>
> *Jude* 20, 21

Praying in the Spirit keeps the believer in the love of God—that love which bears and endures *all* things. Therefore, when any believer gets offended, it is a clear indication that his love is not yet perfected.

The time of temptation to be offended should be a time of self-examination. When one is tempted to be offended, the human tendency is to point at others and blame them for the offense. God wants to teach His children, however, to point at themselves during these times and to search their own hearts to see if they need to be more grounded in His Word and to operate more fully in His love.

"No man hath seen God at any time. If we love one another, God dwelleth in us, and his love is perfected in us"(1 John 4:12). It is only as we believers love one another that the love of God will be able to perform its work in our lives to the extent that it will keep us from getting offended.

The third way to overcome being offended is through ministry. Jesus left us an example of how to overcome hurt feelings through His ministry at the Last Supper. After He washed the disciples' feet, He told them: "...I have given you an example, that ye should do as I have done to you" (John 13:15).

In giving us this example to follow, Jesus knelt down at the feet of Judas, knowing that he would betray Him. Surely our Lord was tempted to be offended with Judas, for the Bible tells us that He "was in all points tempted like as we are, yet without sin" (Hebrews 4:15). He had poured His heart and life into this person for three years, and now this individual was on the verge of betraying Him. Jesus overcame the temptation to be offended by ministering love to the very person who would betray Him to His death. "But I say unto you, Love your enemies, bless them that curse you, do good to them that hate you, and pray for them which despitefully use you, and persecute you" (Matthew 5:44).

Jesus taught this principle because He knew that love will be perfected in the lives of believers who minister to those who have the greatest power to offend them. In these instances, believers who dwell on self will get offended, but those who force themselves to minister to their betrayers and abusers will overcome the temptation to be offended.

For example, suppose a believer prays fervently for someone who is persecuting him through slanderous criticism. Because of his prayer, this believer supernaturally experiences an overwhelming sense of the love of God for his persecutor, thus freeing him from all thoughts of offense. The end result will be good for both parties involved. That is God's plan for the perfection of the saint as well as the salvation of the sinner.

The temptation to be offended will be always be there because we believers are only human. However, as we learn to minister to those who abuse us, we will walk spiritually free from the restraining satanic tool of hurt feelings. Replacing hurt feelings with the love of God frustrates the plan of the enemy and implements the plan of God.

The Lord Jesus taught us to minister to those who abuse us, not only for their sakes, but also for ours. His words are echoed by the Apostle Paul in his letter to the believers in Rome:

Dearly beloved, avenge not yourselves, but rather give place unto wrath: for it is written, Vengeance is mine; I will repay, saith the Lord. Therefore if thine enemy hunger, feed him; if he thirst, give him drink: for in so doing thou shalt heap coals of fire on his head. Be not overcome of evil, but overcome evil with good.

Romans 12:19–21

Many believers are being overcome of evil. When persecutions, afflictions, and trials come their way, their dispositions change, and they are overcome. God wants His children to turn the tables on the enemy, however, and to overcome the evil they encounter with good. This will begin when we believers stop thinking of ourselves and start learning how to minister the love of God to all those we feel tempted to be offended by. Not only will this action benefit those who have a quarrel with us, it will also benefit us.

Believers who find fault in their ministers should earnestly pray for them. Prayer changes the heart of the one who prays as much as it changes the one prayed for. If we believers would pray for one another as much as we criticize one another, then our love for each other and witness to the world would increase. Overcoming offense is one way we obey the command of Jesus in John 13:34–35:

A new commandment I give unto you, That ye love one another; as I have loved you, that ye also love one another. By this shall all men know that ye are my disciples, if ye have love one to another.

Another major bushel in the Body of Christ today is intimidation. This should not be, "For God hath not given us the spirit of fear; but of power, and of love, and of a sound mind" (2 Timothy 1:7). This word translated fear is the Greek word *delelia* (*di-lee'-ah*), and actually means "*timidity.*" God has not given us believers a timid or shy spirit.

Timidity is a thief that robs us of our potential for goodness. It will have an adverse effect on the power, love, and sound mind which have been promised us by God. If we are timid toward people, then we cannot possibly love them as we should.

A believer cannot have a sound mind when he is timid, neither will he be as powerful as God intends for him to be: "The wicked flee when no man pursueth: but the righteous are bold as a lion" (Proverbs 28:1). If a Christian is righteous, then he should also be bold, for God intended that His children be blessed with both righteousness and boldness. Quite often, however, a Christian will read Proverbs 28:1 and reason within himself, "oh well, one out of two isn't bad." We believers have a right to both righteousness and boldness, but sometimes we must battle timidity in order to claim our rightful inheritance.

Timidity will also hinder the fruit of kindness from developing in a believer's life. Many Christians have a beautiful spirit of kindness but because of timidity, that spirit does not always come forth. Many times, timid people are misunderstood and thought to be rude and conceited, when in reality they are only shy. When it takes a long time to get to know a person before the gentle spirit of kindness within him will finally manifest itself, then that person suffers from timidity. He needs to develop some "holy boldness."

The first way to become bold is to spend time in the presence of Jesus. God wants His children to be "bold as lions" (Proverbs 28:1) so that they will be able to express His loving kindness to people. In order to be like lions, however, believers must spend time with the lion. Those who associate with "dogs" (as unbelievers are called in Matthew 7:6), will come to act like dogs, but those who associate with lions will come to act like lions. Therefore, believers in need of boldness should spend time in the presence of the Lion of the Tribe of Judah:

> *Now when they saw the boldness of Peter and John, and perceived that they were unlearned and ignorant men, they marveled; and they took knowledge of them, that they had been with Jesus.*
>
> *Acts 4:13*

The reason Peter and John possess such boldness is that they had been with the Lion: "The lion hath roared, who will not fear? The Lord God hath spoken, who can but prophesy?" (Amos 3:8). Who can help but speak when the Lion roars?

There will always be the temptation to be intimidated by certain circumstances and certain people, but when we believers get in the presence of the Lion and clearly hear Him roar, we cannot help but speak up—whatever our surroundings.

The problem with most people who suffer from timidity is that they are too hesitant to speak forth what the Lord is saying to their hearts. However, when believers know that what they have heard inside is truly the voice of the Lion, then they will be bold to speak it forth clearly and confidently. In order to hear the voice of the Lion, however, it is necessary to take time to listen to the Spirit within.

The second way we believers can become bold is simply by asking God for boldness. Did not James tell us: "...ye have not, because ye ask not" (James 4:2)? We should learn to ask our heavenly Father for boldness and a manifestation of His power. This is exactly what the disciples of Jesus did in Acts 4:29–30:

> *And now, Lord, behold their threatenings: and grant unto thy servants, that with all boldness they may speak thy word, By stretching forth thine hand to heal; and that signs and wonders may be done by the name of thy holy child Jesus.*

And what was the result of their prayer?

> *And when they had prayed, the place was shaken where they were assembled together; and they were all filled with the Holy Ghost, and they spake the word of God with boldness.*
>
> *Acts 4:31*

God answered the disciples' prayer and gave them so much boldness that the room they were in was shaken!

We should never hesitate to ask God for boldness, neither should we be afraid of receiving something other than what we have requested. If we ask God for boldness, will He give us shyness? "Or what man is there of you, whom if his son ask bread, will he give him a stone? Or if he ask a fish, will he give him a serpent?" (Matthew 7:9, 10). Our Lord encourages us to ask of Him because He has a Father's heart that desires to give good things to His children: "If ye then, being evil, know how to give good gifts unto your children, how much more shall your Father which is in heaven give good things to them that ask him?" (v. 11).

Timidity is a very frustrating spirit. Timid believers know what God is speaking to their hearts for them to do; they may even step out to do it, but because of their timidity they will back off at their first sign of opposition, difficulty, or embarrassment. Such people need to ask God for boldness just as the disciples did in Acts 4:29–30. God will answer that prayer today just as he answered it then. He wants His people to be as bold as lions.

The third way we believers can become bold is by praying for one another:

Praying always with all prayer and supplication in the Spirit, and watching thereunto with all perseverance and supplication for all saints; And for me, that utterance may be given unto me, that I may open my mouth boldly, to make known the mystery of the gospel, For which I am an ambassador in bonds: that therein I may speak boldly, as I ought to speak.

Ephesians 6:18–20

The life and death of Jesus was the manifestation of God's kindness and goodness to the world. We, His followers, must develop the fruits of gentleness and goodness in our lives if we are ever to be like our Lord and Savior. The manifestations of His gentleness—that is, His works of goodness—comprise the major portion of the Gospels. His gentleness may be detected in His words: "be of good comfort" (Matthew 9:22), "so have I loved you" (John 15:9), "be not afraid" (Matthew 14:27), "weep not" (Luke 7:13), and "Be of good cheer" (Matthew 14:27). His corresponding acts of goodness may be detected when He cleansed the leper (Luke 17:14), healed the sick (Matthew 4:24), and raised the dead (John 11:44).

His kindness preceded His goodness, which preceded His teaching, for it fertilized the hearts of the hearers to receive the Word. His kindness was obvious, for the little dusty villages emptied themselves when He passed through, and "there followed him great multitudes of people" (Matthew 4:25).

According to Mark 3:8–10, it was His goodness that wooed the crowds to the sea where they heard Him teach and saw Him heal the sick: "...a great multitude, when they had heard what great things he did, came unto him" (v. 8). They followed Him across the hills where they heard Him teach and saw Him break the bread that was to satisfy their hunger (Mark 8:1–8). They followed

Him throughout His life wherever He went—across the sea, the hills, the plains—observed His kindness and goodness and listened to Him teach. They could not let Him go, so they followed Him to the cross where they heard His word: "Father, forgive them; for they know not what they do" (Luke 23:34).

Jesus was always kind to the people, and He ever did acts of goodness on their behalf. Therefore, if we today would be like Jesus, we must begin by being kind.

EXCELLENCE OF SPIRIT

"But the fruit of the Spirit is...faith..."

Galatians 5:22

The best translation of the Greek word rendered faith in the King James Version is actually the word *"faithfulness."* Since all believers are hoping one day to hear the Lord say to them personally and individually, "Well done, thou good and faithful servant" (Matthew 25:21), this particular fruit of the Spirit is very important for us to consider and cultivate. We find a good example of faithfulness in the Old Testament:

> *It pleased Darius to set over the kingdom a hundred and twenty princes, which should be over the whole kingdom; And over these three presidents; of whom Daniel was first: that the princes might give accounts unto them, and the king should have no damage. Then this Daniel was preferred above the presidents and princes, because an excellent spirit was in him; and the king thought to set him over the whole realm.*
>
> *Daniel 6:1–3*

Daniel was a man of an "excellent spirit." This word excellent, in the Hebrew, means *"preeminent"* or "outstanding." Daniel had such an excellent spirit about him that he just stood out from all the others around him.

What was it about Daniel that caused him to be so noticeably different from the rest? What is it in some children of God today which causes them to stand out from the others? In every church there are certain believers who seem to be discernably more prominent than their fellow Christians. Certainly, all believers should desire to develop an excellent spirit and be preeminent. So many, however, seem to be content with just being nominal church members. Those who desire to please their heavenly Father by being of an excellent spirit can learn how to accomplish this by studying the life of Daniel.

> *Then the presidents and princes sought to find occasion against Daniel concerning the kingdom; but they could find none occasion nor fault; forasmuch as he was faithful, neither was there any error or fault found in him.*
>
> *Daniel 6:4*

It was *faithfulness* that caused Daniel to stand out from all the others.

"Most men will proclaim every one his own goodness: but a faithful man who can find?" (Proverbs 20:6). It is difficult to find a truly faithful person today. Yet if there is any one characteristic or virtue that causes a person to stand out from the crowd and to receive God's undivided attention, it is faithfulness.

The Lord spoke through the Psalmist David saying: "Mine eyes shall be upon the faithful of the land, that they may dwell with me: he that walketh in a perfect way, he shall serve me" (Psalm 101:6). When the Lord finds a faithful believer, He focuses His undivided attention upon him. Therefore, we believers should desire to develop the fruit of faithfulness because God is looking for this character quality in His people.

The first function of the fruit of faithfulness is to equip believers to exercise stewardship over God's goods:

> *These are the generations of the heavens and of the earth when they were created, in the day that the LORD God made the earth and the heavens, And every plant of the field before it was in the earth, and every herb of the field before it grew: for the LORD God had not caused it to rain upon the earth, and there was not a man to till the ground. But there went up a mist from the earth, and watered the whole face of the ground. And the LORD God formed man of the dust of the ground, and breathed into his nostrils the breath of life; and man became a living soul. And the LORD God planted a garden eastward in Eden; and there he put the man whom he had formed. And the LORD God took the man, and put him into the Garden of Eden to dress it and to keep it.*
>
> *Genesis 2:4–8, 15*

God created Adam for fellowship, but there was another reason for the creation of man. God had created the heavens and the earth; the mist came up out of the ground and watered the earth, causing it to produce plants and herbs. But there was no one to till the ground. Therefore, according to verse 15, the original reason God made man was so he could care for the Garden of Eden. So God made man not only for fellowship, but also for the purpose of being a recipient of, and ruler over, His creation. This is not just true of Adam in the beginning; today God is still looking for faithful men to whom He can entrust His goods.

> *Therefore the* LORD *God sent him forth from the garden of Eden, to till the ground from whence he was taken. So he drove out the man; and he placed at the east of the garden of Eden Cherubims, and a flaming sword which turned every way, to keep the way of the tree of life.*
>
> *Genesis 3:23, 24*

Man's unfaithfulness caused God to drive him out from that which he was to rule over. This is the reason God wants to develop faithfulness in believers today—so they will not lose the privilege of ruling over the things He has for them in the Spirit.

God will bless His people individually with as much as He can trust them to responsibly administer. But because of their unfaithfulness, God cannot entrust too many people the gifts of the Spirit, the wisdom, the knowledge, and the revelations contained in His Word.

It is only the faithful who are ever fully entrusted with continuous rule over God's choicest goods: "A faithful man shall abound with blessings..." (Proverbs 28:20).

> *Who then is a faithful and wise servant, whom his lord hath made ruler over his household, to give them meat in due season? Blessed is that servant, whom his lord when he cometh shall find so doing. Verily I say unto you, That he shall make him ruler over all his goods.*
>
> *Matthew 24:45–47*

The parable of the talents in Matthews 25:14–30 compares the kingdom of heaven with a man who entrusted his servants with his goods before traveling into a far country. To one he gave five talents, to another two talents, and to the third he gave one talent. Then he went on his journey.

When he returned, the master called for an accounting from his servants. He commended the good and faithful servants who had invested what was entrusted to them and presented him an increase. The servant entrusted with five talents presented his lord with ten talents and heard him speak the words, "Well done, thou good and faithful servant" (v. 21). The servant entrusted with two talents presented his lord with four and also heard the words, "Well done, good and faithful servant" (v. 23)

The servant with the one talent, however, admitted that he had not been faithful with his lord's goods in that he had fearfully taken the one talent entrusted to him and had hidden in the ground. The response of the lord to the unfaithful servant is a spiritual warning of which every believer who is serving the Lord Jesus should be aware.

> *Take therefore the talent from him, and give it unto him which hath ten talents. For unto every one that hath shall be given, and he shall have abundance: but from him that hath not shall be taken away even that which he hath.*
>
> Matthew 25:28, 29

It is a spiritual principle that God will take His goods from the unfaithful and give them to the faithful. According to verse 29, every one who has been faithful will receive more, but he who has been unfaithful will lose even what he does have. Verse 28 indicates that his goods will be taken from him by the Lord and bestowed upon someone who will use them wisely for the sake of the Lord's kingdom. Therefore, if we believers today are not faithful with what God has entrusted to us, then He will take it from us and give it to those who are faithful.

Some Charismatic believers seem to think that they have no gifts, but this is not so. The word charismatic comes from the Greek word *charisma* which is composed of two Greek root words meaning "a gift" and "favor, grace." So then all "Charismatics"—all Spirit-filled believers—have been entrusted with God's "gifts of grace." Those who are faithful with their assigned gifts will abound with God's goods; they will experience an abundant harvest of God's wisdom, knowledge, revelation, and blessings.

In Hebrews 12:12–13 we are warned of the dangers of unfaithfulness:

> *Wherefore lift up the hands which hang down, and the feeble knees; And make straight paths for your feet, lest that which is lame be turned out of the way; but let it rather be healed.*

The writer of Hebrews then cites the case of Jacob and Esau as an example of the spiritual principle of the blessings being taken from the unfaithful and given to the faithful: "Lest there be any fornicator, or profane person, as Esau, who for one morsel of meat sold his birthright" (Hebrews 12: 16). Since he was the firstborn son, Esau was supposed to be the one to inherit the family blessing from his father, Isaac. The birthright was taken from him, however, and given to his younger brother Jacob because Esau did not have a faithful heart. In God's providence, it was always planned that way, of course, but legally Esau lost his birthright because it was not his heart's desire to be faithful to God.

We read of a similar forfeiture of a spiritual blessing in the case of Saul: "But the spirit of the Lord departed from Saul, and an evil spirit from the Lord troubled him" (1 Samuel 16:14). The Lord chose Saul to serve as king of Israel. However, when he proved himself unfaithful to that calling, the Lord removed His anointing and placed it upon David, the young shepherd boy He knew would be faithful.

The Lord Jesus referred to this principle when He told the people of His day: "Therefore say I unto you, The kingdom of God shall be taken from you, and given to a nation bringing forth the fruits thereof" (Matthew 21:43). The nation of Israel was not faithful with the revelation of the promised Messiah, so the Lord took that revelation from them and gave it to the Gentiles, a people who would accept it and be faithful to it.

"For the gifts and calling of God are without repentance" (Romans 11:29). This applies to those believers who once made a commitment to the Lord and were living for Him but who have since backslidden, thus losing the anointing that was upon them. If they will repent and return to the Lord, the anointing of the Lord will return upon them, for God's gifts and calling are without repentance (irrevocable).

Those believers who are not faithful with their God-given gifts, however, are in danger of losing them.

There are those in the Body of Christ who have the gift of intercession, yet they refuse to utilize it. There are those who have the gift of the word of knowledge but will not bring it forth. There are those who have the gift of prophecy but are too lazy to stir up the gift by praying in the Spirit before they come to church services. There are those who have an anointing to teach God's Word but simply will not take the time to get into that Word and dig out the treasures of wisdom and knowledge which are contained in it. There are those whom God has given the priceless Baptism of the Holy Spirit but who neglect praying in tongues.

It is definitely a spiritual principle that God will take the gifts from those who are unfaithful and give them to those who are faithful. If they are not careful, such unfaithful servants may one day find themselves in the same sad position as Esau: "For ye know how that afterward, when he would have inherited the blessing, he was rejected: for he found no place of repentance, though he sought it carefully with tears" (Hebrews 12:17).

There was once a believer who had a tremendous anointing for the word of knowledge. He could just look at people and discern their innermost thoughts. Because of his gift, he knew every sin his wife had ever committed. His gifts was so awesome, he felt overwhelmed by it.

One day this man was fellowshipping with another minister. He began to speak of the "burden" of his gift remarking, "I wsh God would take this gift from me because I just can't handle it." His wish was granted. It wasn't long afterward that the Lord did remove that gift from him.

Later on, the man progressed in his walk with the Lord. After he had become more spiritually mature he wished he had not been so hasty in rejecting the Lord's gift. He began to cry out for God to restore it to him, but so far it has not been returned to him.

There is a double lesson here for us believers. First of all, we need to be very careful to be faithful in appreciating and exercising whatever gift(s) the Lord chooses to bestow upon us. Secondly, we should learn to earnestly desire spiritual gifts.

When the man said that he did not want the gift God had given him, the minister with whom he was fellowshipping instantly prayed under his breath, "Lord, I'll take it!" That prayer was pleasing to the Lord. Our heavenly Father is looking for faithful people on whom He can abundantly bestow His gifts. He will take the gifts from the unfaithful and the unappreciative to bestow them upon those who will appreciate and utilize them. Their desire and faithfulness will produce an abundance of blessings for them and for those to whom they minister.

In 1 Corinthians 12:31 we see that God has given us believers an open invitation to "covet earnestly the best gifts." This invitation is recorded for a reason; it is presented so God can bestow these precious gifts upon those who sincerely desire them enough to seek after them with all their heart. Instead of using all our faith to obtain material possessions, we believers should be exercising faith for the acquisition of the gifts of the Spirit. All these other things would be added to us as well, but in addition we would find ourselves abounding in the "true riches."

The second function of the fruit of faithfulness is to enable believers to experience fellowship with the Father:

And Miriam and Aaron spake against Moses because of the Ethiopian woman whom he had married: for

*he had married an Ethiopian woman. And they said,
Hath the LORD indeed spoken only by Moses? hath he
not spoken also by us? And the LORD heard it. And the
LORD came down in the pillar of the cloud, and stood
in the door of the tabernacle, and called Aaron and
Miriam: and they both came forth. And he said, Hear
now my words: If there be a prophet among you, I the
LORD will make myself known unto him in a vision,
and will speak unto him in a dream. My servant Moses
is not so, who is faithful in all mine house. With him
will I speak mouth to mouth, even apparently, and not
in dark speeches; and the similitude of the LORD shall
he behold: wherefore then were ye not afraid to speak
against my servant Moses?*

Numbers 1, 2, 5–8

Verse 8 describes the result of Moses' faithfulness—God
spoke to him "mouth to mouth, even apparently." In
the Hebrew, the word translated "apparently" means
clear or manifest to the understanding. Because of the
faithfulness of Moses, God's voice was very clear and
manifest to his understanding.

How often Christians express the fact that they just
cannot hear the voice of God clearly. They complain
that, to them, God's voice is muffled and so difficult
to understand. These believers should honestly examine
their faithfulness, for the Word says because Moses was
faithful God spoke to him in a clear voice that was completely understandable to his mind.

Jesus said: "I can of mine own self do nothing: as I
hear, I judge: and my judgment is just; because I seek

not mine own will, but the will of the Father which hath sent me" (John 5:30). Jesus had such an intimate relationship with the Father that every time He was faced with a situation, He clearly heard the voice of God and immediately discerned what to do.

For example, when the Jews brought to Him the woman taken in adultery and wanted to stone her, Jesus heard the voice of God and stooped down and began to write on the ground what God had told Him to write (John 8:3–11). Because Jesus heard the voice of God clearly and knew exactly how to respond to that situation, the scribes and Pharisees became convicted of their own sinfulness and gradually left, one by one.

In John 8:26, Jesus said: "I have many things to say and to judge of you: but he that sent me is true; and I speak to the world those things which I have heard of him." God's voice was so clear and apparent to Jesus that the words He spoke were the exact words of the Father.

Wherefore, holy brethren, partakers of the heavenly calling, consider the Apostle and High Priest of our profession, Christ Jesus; Who was faithful to him that appointed him, as also Moses was faithful in all his house.

Hebrews 3:1, 2

The reason Jesus was able to hear the Father's voice so clearly was because He was faithful. Hebrews 3:2 compares the faithfulness of Jesus with the faithfulness of Moses. Jesus received the same benefit of having the

Father speak to Him clearly and distinctly as Moses did. We believers today will perceive the clarity of God's voice only as we are faithful to obey His commands and thus fulfill His will.

Jesus told His disciples: "My sheep hear my voice, and I know them, and they follow me" (John 10:27). Believers are not faithful to follow because they hear the voice of the Good Shepherd; rather, they hear the Good Shepherd's voice because they are faithful. The word faithfulness in the Greek means "*trustworthy*" or "*trustful.*" God does not speak to believers just so they can say they have heard His voice; He speaks to those He knows He can trust to follow Him.

One advantage God has over His children is that He knows them, even better than they know themselves. He will not utter His voice to one of them just so He can go out and proclaim, "I heard from God! I heard from God! Glory be, I got a goose bump!" Instead, God will speak to those He knows will follow Him out of obedience. It is only as we believers develop a faithful and obedient heart that God can trust us to hear His voice.

God is looking for those to whom He can speak in the middle of the night and say, "Get up and pray," as they will obediently get out of bed and get on their knees. Our Lord does not say, "Get up and pray," just so a person can wake up the next morning rejoicing in how wonderful it was that God spoke to him during the night. God will only speak clearly to the person who will be obedient to His voice once he has heard it.

Neither will God tell a believer to go down the street

and witness to his neighbor, just so that believer can boast of how God spoke to him and gave him an order. God speaks directly to a person for one reason: so that person will do what he has been told to do. If he is not willing to be obedient, then he won't hear from God for very long. The Lord doesn't waste His time talking to people who don't listen or obey.

God knows His children. He knows which of them will follow the leading voice. In these end times, those whom God knows to be faithful are about to become very busy indeed, because the Lord is going to be speaking a great deal.

God told one minister, "When you pray, wear your shoes!" This is the Lord's message to all who are faithful, for there is much work to be done in these last days—and few laborers willing to do it.

The third function of the fruit of faithfulness is to enable believers to experience the joy of pleasing the Father. In reference to the day all believers will stand before Him to be rewarded for their deeds, Jesus said that the faithful will be told: "Well done, thou good and faithful servant: thou hast been faithful over a few things, I will make thee ruler over many things: enter thou into the joy of thy Lord" (Matthew 25:21). From the Lord's response, we can see that faithfulness on the part of a believer produces joy and appreciation within the heart of his Master.

In John 8:29 Jesus said that He always did those things which *pleased* His Father. In other words, Jesus was always faithful. It should be the heart's desire of every believer to please the Father in everything he says and does. It will only be through faithfulness that we can ever hope to accomplish this.

Being faithful to God should be the most important goal in the life of a Christian, yet so many times we become so busy doing things for God that we are merely doing our own works in His name. Actually, God is more interested in faithfulness than He is in accomplishment. His concern is not how much His children achieve in life as much as it is whether or not they are doing what He has told them to do.

If all God ever told a believer to do was to go somewhere and minister to one certain person for the rest of his life in order to see that individual come to Jesus, then that one act is what would please God most. If this believer were to run off somewhere else and start a huge successful church instead, then he would not be faithful and thus would not be pleasing to his heavenly Father.

God is more concerned about our being faithful to what He is telling us to do than He is in our doing what we think is fruitful. When we stand before the Lord Jesus, the righteous Judge, we won't be able to say, "Lord, look at all I've done," Rather, our Lord will be asking us, "Did you do what I told you to do? Were you faithful?"

"As the cold of snow in the times of harvest, so is a faithful messenger to them that send him: for he refresheth the soul of his masters" (Proverbs 25:13). God is totally refreshed when He finds a faithful messenger. We believers need to realize that our lives can be a blessing to God and minister to Him. When His children are faithful, even in the little things, the heart of God is refreshed, and He is pleased and blessed.

According to the New Testament, *faith* pleases God: "but without faith it is impossible to please him: for he that cometh to God must believe that he is, and that he is a rewarder of them that diligently seek him" (Hebrews 11:6). According to the Apostle Paul, "the just shall live by faith" (Romans 1:7). In other words, the just are to live by pleasing God. Romans 1:17 is a quote of Habakkuk 2:4: "Behold...the just shall live by his faith." In the Hebrew the word translated faith in this verse actually means "*firmness; fidelity:*" or "faithfulness."

Most Christians would be surprised to learn that the English word *faith* appears only two times in the entire King James Version of the Old Testament—here in this verse and in Deuteronomy 32:20. Both times it is used, it refers not to faith as we think of it, but to *faithfulness.* Therefore, many believers read Chapter 11 of the book of Hebrews, which chronicles the exploits of the Old Testament saints of God, and marvel at the great faith of these men of old. In reality, what is being emphasized in that passage is not their great faith, but how they pleased God because of their great *faithfulness!*

Many believers today have made a "golden calf" out of faith. Their attitude seems to be: "Let's develop our faith so we can get all these great things!" Those who have this viewpoint have lost sight of the root meaning of the word *faith,* which is "faithfulness."

Each of us should individually examine himself on

this matter by answering the question, "*Why* do I stand on God's Word when I go through a trial?" If it is for the soul purpose of getting some personal desire fulfilled, then our motive is not to please God. On the other hand, if we stand firm on God's Word because we know that, by doing so, we are being faithful and are pleasing our Father, then our motive is pure.

This is the reason many Christians grow weary of standing in faith during their trials, they are not standing to please God; they are standing to get a desired result. While they are standing on God's Word, their eyes are more on the manifestation of the answer to their need than on their faithful obedience to His Word. As such, they are more concerned with gratifying their own desire than they are with accomplishing God's will (Proverbs 25:13). As a result, when that desired result does not manifest itself in a week or two, they back off and try some other approach. Usually they fall back on the arm of flesh, because all they ever wanted was to obtain some result that would spare them from suffering or deliver them from some trial.

The Church of Jesus Christ must come to understand that the word *faith* means "*faithfulness*" and that the only reason to stand in faith is that by so doing, we are being faithful to God and pleasing Him. It is time to rid the Church of this stereotype of faith, this "golden calf," by which one can supposedly get whatever he wants simply by approaching it with all the right formulas. The Church must understand that faith is the only way anyone can every truly please God the Father.

It is time we believers got our eyes off the results of our faith and onto the will and plan of God for our lives. Then, as trials become worse and worse, we will be able to stand and to continue to stand, because our heart's desire is not to satisfy our lusts but to please our heavenly Father (James 4:3).

Faithfulness enables a child of God to experience the joy of pleasing His father. This is one way we believers can fulfill the commandment of James 1:2, 3 even as our faith is being tried: "My brethren, count it all joy when ye fall into divers temptations; Knowing this, that the trying of your faith worketh patience." Joy will rise up in the hearts of those who know they are pleasing God.

All believers have the seed of faithfulness within their spirits, but they must learn to develop it both as individuals and as the Body of Christ as a whole. Developing a trust between ourselves and God so that we know the Lord trusts us and has faith in us is a beautiful thought indeed.

The first way in which we may cultivate and develop the fruit of faithfulness is by being faithful in that which is least. Jesus said: "He that is faithful in that which is least is faithful also in much: and he that is unjust in the least is unjust also in much" (Luke 16:10). The word *least* is not used here in the sense of lesser importance as compared with everything which exists, but in the sense of the least of that which a person already has in his possession.

It is a very strong spiritual principle that when a believer demonstrates his faithfulness with the least of his possessions, God can then bestow more important possessions upon him. Possessions increase as a person's proven responsibility increases. It is only after an individual has shown himself to be faithful with what he already has that God can trust him enough to bestow more upon him.

On the other hand, many believers are asking God for more faith, more wisdom, and more discernment. They are individually crying out to God, "Give *me* the gift of intercession." "Oh God, give *me* the gift of the word of knowledge." "Father, give *me* the gift of teaching." "Lord, *I* want to teach; *I* want to preach." They are sincerely crying out to God for these things, but in reality they would not even use the things they are so earnestly asking of God.

Our Lord taught that the person who is not faithful with his current possessions cannot be trusted with more. This is a very basic principle, yet believers constantly strive for the "big" things when they are not even faithful yet in the "little" things.

The first area that might be considered least in which believers must be faithful is the fulfillment of past vows to God:

> *When thou vowest a vow unto God, defer not to pay it; for he hath no pleasure in fools: pay that which thou hast vowed. Better is it that thou shouldest not vow, than that thou shouldest vow and not pay. Suffer not thy mouth to cause thy flesh to sin; neither say thou before the angel, that it was an error: wherefore*

should God be angry at thy voice, and destroy the work of thine hands?

Ecclesiastes 5:4–6

At one time or another, every believer has vowed a vow unto God, but not everyone has kept that vow. This is not a light thing to God. So many have said, "Oh Lord, I'm going to witness to every person I see"—and that witnessing lasted for a day or two. So many have said, "Oh Lord, I'm going to fast for a week"—and that fast lasted about two days. So many have promised the Lord that they would do this or that, and then only partially fulfilled their vows.

According to Ecclesiastes 4:6, God will destroy the efforts of these foolish individuals, yet they are crying out to Him for more and more and more. God will not build upon anything that He says in His Word He is going to destroy.

We Christians need to learn to fulfill our vows to God. This is where the Holy Spirit will play a part in our individual lives as He quickens to us our past vows to the Lord that are in need of fulfillment. As the Holy Spirit does His work, may we individual believers be careful not to say, "I didn't mean it, God"; which is just another way of saying, "it was an error" (Ecclesiastes 5:6). Instead, may we be very careful to be faithful in that which is least—such as our past vows to God. If we will be faithful in that which is least, God will begin to give us much.

The second area that might be considered least in which believers must be faithful is their family life:

> *And the men rose up from thence, and looked toward Sodom: and Abraham went with them to bring them on the way. And the LORD said, Shall I hide from Abraham that thing which I do; Seeing that Abraham shall surely become a great and mighty nation, and all the nations of the earth shall be blessed in him?*
>
> *Genesis 18:16–18*

Abraham was a man to whom God entrusted much. In fact, the Lord told Abraham that through his seed *all* nations would be blessed. That is indeed a trustworthy relationship. According to verse 17, God had such a relationship with the man that He would not begin the destruction of Sodom until He had first talked it over with His friend, Abraham.

In verse 19 of that passage, God reveals the reason for His great trust in Abraham. The Lord said: "For I know him, that he will command his children and his household after him, and they shall keep the way of the Lord, to do justice and judgment; that the Lord may bring upon Abraham that which he hath spoken of him." The reason God was able to trust Abraham with much is because he was faithful in that which was least; Abraham was faithful in the area of his family.

There are men of God today who are saying that they need to go out and teach the nations of the earth, yet no doors seem to be opening for them. Still, they express the desire to go out to the ends of the earth and teach and preach Jesus. God is saying to them, "What about your family? *Start with your own family!*"

Husbands must individually ask themselves, "Do I love my wife as Christ loved the Church?" (Ephesians 5:25) Men may be asking God for more knowledge, more wisdom, and more discernment; if so, God is asking them in return, "Do you love your wife as Christ loved the Church?"

Wives must individually ask themselves, "Am I subject to my husband in everything as the Church is subject unto Christ?" (Ephesians 5:24). Women may be asking God for various gifts of the Spirit; if so, God is asking them, "Are you subject to your husband in *every* thing?"

Parents who are looking for a ministry together should ask themselves, "Are we training up our children in the way they should go?" (Proverbs 22:6). God is concerned about the children of believers. He does not want parents sending children to Sunday school as their sole source of instruction about His Word; He wants parents to teach their children themselves. Parents may be asking God for places to go and minister; if so, He is asking them, "Are you training up your children in the way they should go?"

Children must individually ask themselves, "Am I obeying my parents in the Lord?" (Ephesians 6:1). Children may be asking God for more and more; if so, God is asking them, "Are you obeying your parents?"

The third area that might be considered least in which believers must be faithful is their work. Jesus said: "And if ye have not been faithful in that which is another man's, who shall give you what which is your own?" (Luke 16:12) Our lord was simply saying that if we believers are not faithful with those things that other men (such as our employers) have committed to our trust, then God cannot give us that which is our own.

"Servants, obey in all things your masters according to the flesh; not with eye service, as men pleasers; but in singleness of heart, fearing God; And whatsoever ye do, do it heartily, as to the Lord, and not unto men" (Colossians 3:22, 23). We believers need to evaluate our lives to see if we are fulfilling this commandment, for God is definitely concerned about our work habits. We should not begin asking God for more things until we are faithful with what we already have.

For example, there was once a college student who complained to a minister, "You know, I am really discouraged because God never opens any doors for me to preach."

The minister responded in amazement, "God never opens any doors for you to preach?"

"That's right," the young man replied. "No one ever calls and asks me to preach in his church."

"I know you are a college student," the minister said. "How many street corners would you say there are on your college campus?"

The young man gave him a rough estimate, and the minister told him, "Every single one of those street corners is an open door for you to preach; God won't open doors for you until you've gone through the ones that are open before you where you are right now."

This principle is true of any area of life. God will begin to add opportunities to believers' lives when they are faithful to take advantage of those opportunities already available to them.

The second way in which believers may develop the fruit of faithfulness is by being faithful with money, that which the Bible refers to as "unrighteous mammon" (Luke 16:11) and "filthy lucre" (1 Timothy 3:3). There is an uncanny correlation between a person's faithfulness to God and his attitude toward money. Jesus said: "If therefore ye have not been faithful in the unrighteous mammon, who will commit to your trust the true riches?" (Luke 16:11). A person who maintains a scriptural attitude toward money is a person whom God can trust with the "true riches," which are spiritual prosperity.

There is no other substance on the face of the earth which alienates people's affections from God more than money. This is why Jesus said: "No servant can serve two masters: for either he will hate the one, and love the other; or else he will hold to the one, and despise the other. Ye cannot serve God and mammon" (Luke 16:13). Notice He did not say, "you cannot serve God and football" (or any other interest or concern). He said, "You cannot serve God and *money.*"

Being God, Jesus said this because He knew that money would be the main cause of separation between people and their Creator. There are three ways money separates people's affections from God. The first way is in their thoughts.

It is amazing how much the subject of money occupies the minds of many believers. They constantly think such thoughts as: "How will the bills be paid?" "Where is the money coming from for us to live?" "If the cost of living keeps going up, how will we be able to make ends meet?" Such thoughts continually flood the minds of countless otherwise faithful believers, preventing them from setting their affections totally on God. Since money will play such an important role in these end times, believers must take the following words of Jesus seriously and develop the proper attitude toward money:

> *But seek ye first the kingdom of God, and his righteousness; and all these things shall be added unto you. Take therefore no thought for the morrow: for the morrow shall take thought for the things of itself. Sufficient unto the day is the evil thereof.*
>
> *Matthew 6: 33, 34*

The second way in which money separates people's affections from God is in their time. Our Lord taught His disciples: "Labour not for the meat which perisheth, but for that meat which endureth unto everlasting life, which the Son of man shall give unto you: for him hath God the Father sealed" (John 6:27). One of the biggest snares of the enemy is to get believers working so much that, in essence, their time is spent working only for "filthy lucre" and not for "that meat which endureth everlasting life."

Time is very valuable to God, and since the only time that men possess is the present, it should be considered valuable by them as well. This is why the Apostle Paul admonishes us to redeem the time (Ephesians 5:16).

The third way in which money separates people's affection from God is in their accumulation and possession of it: "Every man according as he purposeth in his heart, so let him give; not grudgingly, or of necessity: for God loveth a cheerful giver" (2 Corinthians 9:7). When many believers hear teaching on giving, they enter into a "grudge match" with God. Admittedly, they will usually finally succumb and give, but they do so grudgingly. Then they struggle with thoughts of regret and resentment for a week or two because they did break down and give. This is a clear indication that such people have great affection for money; affection for money will alienate their affection from God.

Money itself is not evil; the evil lies in the affection people have for it: "For the love of money is the root of all evil: which while some coveted after, they have erred from the faith, and pierced themselves through with many sorrows" (1 Timothy 6:10).

Too many believers have the attitude toward their money, "Ninety percent of it is mine to do with as I please." When God directs them to give more than the standard ten percent, they either give grudgingly, or not at all. The problem is that they have affection for money. God cannot trust such people with the "true riches."

On the other hand, when God speaks to faithful believers' hearts asking them to give the tithe and even more, they respond eagerly and cheerfully because they have no real affection for money. God will bestow the "true riches" upon anyone who gives with the attitude, "I'm always happy to give my money to the Lord; after all, it *all* belongs to Him anyhow."

The third, and certainly most important, way in which believers may develop the fruit of faithfulness is by being aware of God's indwelling presence. Jesus said: "And he that sent me is with me: the Father hath not left me alone; for I do always those things that please him" (John 8:29). Jesus knew that He was never alone; He had a conscious awareness of the Father's presence with Him. Because of this, Jesus always did the things that delighted the Father; He pleased God with His faithfulness.

Pleasing the Father by being aware of His indwelling presence may be compared to a father who is teaching his child to ride a bicycle. Dad proudly gets out the brand new two-wheeler and gives his son step-by-step instructions on how to ride it.

"First, get balanced on the seat while I hold it steady," he tells him.

The child obeys and quickly climbs onto the seat, while Dad's firm grip holds the bike upright.

"Don't rock around on it, now. Just put your hands on the handlebars."

The child quits squirming and in excitement grips the handlebars a little too tightly, trying to contain himself as he awaits the big moment.

Dad is very reassuring as he says, "Good. Let's go. Pedal it easy now."

By this time, Dad has given the bike a little push, and the child is doing his best to follow Dad's instruction, but he only goes about three yards before the bicycle wobbles dangerously, and then he falls! Boom!

Dad immediately comes over, picks him up, dusts him off, and speaks word of encouragement. "That's all right, son. Tell you what I'll do—I'll run along behind and hold onto the seat while you ride."

The child gratefully agrees, and once again he is off and pedaling. This time, however, he is doing much better. He is steady, balanced, confident, and moving. He turns his head and looks over his shoulder to show Dad how great he's doing—but Dad is not there!

Boom! He immediately falls.

Dad runs over, picks him up, dusts him off, and says, "Son, I don't understand. You went a full ten yards all by yourself before you realized I wasn't there."

"I know it, but I need to know you're there, Dad."

As long as the child was aware of his father's presence, he remained balanced and steady. As soon as he lost this conscious awareness, however, he fell.

This same principle is true of believers today. Just as the child learning to ride the bicycle fell when he lost the conscious awareness of the presence of his earthly father, we believers stumble and fall when we lose the conscious awareness of the presence of our heavenly Father.

Once believers get the revelation of Christ, the hope of glory (Colossians 1:27), they will suddenly begin to become successful in the things of God. Therefore, we Christians must always be aware of our Father's presence within us if we are to please Him with our faithfulness.

> *And what agreement hath the temple of God with idols? For ye are the temple of the living God; as God hath said, I will dwell in them, and walk in them; and I will be their God, and they shall be my people.*
> *2 Corinthians 6:16*

The worst thing that religious traditions have done is give people the mistaken idea that the Church is a building. God, however, no longer lives in tabernacles made of hands: "Howbeit the most High dwelleth not in temples made with hands..." (Acts 7:48). Rather, God's dwelling is in His children: "Whosoever shall confess that Jesus is the Son of God, God dwelleth in him, and he in God" (1 John 4:15). Believers must get this revelation in their hearts: God, through the presence of the Holy Spirit, has come and made His abode within His people.

"Jesus answered and said unto them, If a man love me, he will keep my words: and my father will love him, and we will come unto him, and make our abode with him" (John 14:23). Notice that Jesus said: "*We* will come and make *our* abode with him." The Father and Son, through the Holy Ghost, have come and taken up residence within the children of God.

If they are ever to succeed in life, the Church of Jesus Christ must have the awareness that they are not alone. This is exactly what Jesus said in John 8:29: "the

Father hath not left me alone" It is amazing; however, how many people in the Body of Christ are "alone." They have such a feeling of insecurity that when they are required to be faithful to the Word and will of God, they become frustrated and ask, "But how will I ever be able to do it?" They are not aware of the fact that there is One living within them to do the work Himself: "For it is God which worketh in you both to will and to do of his good pleasure" (Philippians 2:13).

We believers must get this truth in our hearts. When we were born again, we did not simply become members of a particular church, we became *the* church. Instead of joining a church, we actually became the temple of the living God; God dwells in us by His Holy Spirit. God almighty is in His people. The same Spirit who raised Jesus Christ from the dead dwells in us.

We Christians must realize that this same Spirit can empower us to be faithful to the Word we hear. The resurrecting Spirit of God can empower us today to overcome bad habits in our lives, to quit gossiping about other people, to resist evil of every kind, to hear the Word of the Lord, and to obey that Word. This same Spirit can strengthen us to be faithful in the things He directs us to do. We believers have to know, however, that it is not us against the world, for the Greater One has come to live in us.

Paul had this marvelous revelation. He said: "For in him we live and move, and have our being;...For we are also his offspring" (Acts 17:28). How could any man otherwise have endured such affliction and persecution as

Paul did? Would most believers today honestly stand up to the things Paul suffered? They would not, unless they had his revelation: "Christ in you, the hope of glory" (Colossians 1:27).

When facing persecution and affliction, we believers must receive the revelation that the greater One lives within us personally and individually: "Ye are of God, little children, and have overcome them: because greater is he that is in you, then he that is in the world" (1 John 4:4). Once we fully grasp this truth, we can say with Paul: "What shall we then say to these things? If God be for us, who can be against us?" (Romans 8:31).

Later on in that same chapter, Paul asks: "Who shall separate us from the love of Christ? Shall tribulation, or distress, or persecution, or famine, or nakedness, or peril, or sword?" (Romans 8:35). There can be no such separation, because believers are one spirit with God: "But he that is joined unto the Lord is one spirit" (1 Corinthians 6:17).

A miracle occurs when a person says, "Jesus, I receive You as my Lord and Savior." The miracle is not that he sheds a few tears, nor is it that he finally gets on his knees and says, "Okay, Lord, I give up." The miracle is that by receiving the Lord Jesus Christ into his life, he actually becomes a new person: "Therefore if any man be in Christ, he is a new creature: old things are passed away; behold, all things are become new" (2 Corinthians 5:17).

By receiving the Son of God into his heart, the believer actually becomes the tabernacle, or dwelling place, of the heavenly Father. If God's people only had a full awareness of the indwelling of the Spirit of God within them, their lives would be totally different. They would not say some of the things they say, go some of the places they go, do some of the things they do—for when this truth is in the heart, a person cannot help but walk holy and upright.

God is truly living within His people. He is there to cause them *to will and to do of his good pleasure* (Philippians 2:13).

God is a faithful Father. Whenever His children sin, most of them do not hesitate to fall to their knees and confess their sins to Him. They do not question or worry about whether their heavenly Father will forgive them their sin, for they know He is faithful: "If we confess our sins, he is faithful and just to forgive us our sins, and to cleanse us from all unrighteousness" (1 John 1:9).

What greater knowledge could men possess than to know that in spite of their human faults and weaknesses, God remains faithful to forgive them of their sins and to make them new creatures in Christ? (2 Corinthians 5:17). The assurance that their hearts will be made pure and preserved from the deceit, destruction, and wickedness that is permeating this world should create an appreciative desire within God's children to be faithful in response to the faithfulness of their Father.

May we believers begin to cultivate and develop the fruit of faithfulness in our lives, and may we do so out of hearts abounding in love and appreciation for the faithfulness of our God to His Word.

GREAT MEEKNESS BRINGS GREAT POWER

"But the fruit of the Spirit is...Meekness..."
Galatians 5:22, 23

The biblical definition of the word meekness has often been misunderstood by believers as well as non-believers. Everybody knows that Jesus was meek, and they usually associate meekness with His ability to suffer abuse without resorting to any form of retaliation. Meekness, however, has a three-part definition that includes much more than just this one aspect of non-retaliation A person who is meek is 1) self-controlled or slow to give and take offense, 2) humble in spirit and lowly in mind, and 3) teachable. All three of these attributes make up the fruit of meekness in the life of a believer.

The first function of the fruit of meekness is to enable believers to develop self-control, to be slow to give or take offense:

> *For this is thankworthy, if a man for conscience toward God endure grief, suffering wrongfully. For what glory is it, if, when ye be buffeted for your faults, ye shall*

take it patiently? but if, when ye do well, and suffer for
it, ye take it patiently, this is acceptable with God.

1 *Peter* 2:19–20

Many believers today consider themselves meek if they do not take offense when they are reprimanded for their wrong actions. It is not an opportunity for exhibiting meekness, however, when a person who is at fault suffers the consequences of his own misdeeds. Meekness is displayed when a person does not take offense when he suffers for being in the right.

A truly meek person possesses the self-control to react positively even when he is being falsely accused, slandered, afflicted, or persecuted. The strength to exercise self-control while suffering injustice comes from cultivating the fruit of meekness. A good example of one whose life gave evidence of meekness was Moses:

And Miriam and Aaron spake against Moses because of the Ethiopian woman whom he had married: for he had married an Ethiopian woman. And they said, Hath the LORD indeed spoken only by Moses? hath he not spoken also by us? And the LORD heard it. (Now the man Moses was very meek, above all the men which were upon the face of the earth.) And the LORD spake suddenly unto Moses, and unto Aaron, and unto Miriam, Come out ye three unto the tabernacle of the congregation. And they three came out. And the LORD came down in the pillar of the cloud, and stood in the door of the tabernacle, and called Aaron and Miriam: and they both came forth. And he said, Hear now my words: If there be a prophet among you, I the LORD will make myself known unto him in a vision, and will speak unto him in a dream. My servant Moses is not so, who is faithful in all mine house. With him will I speak mouth to mouth, even apparently, and not in dark speeches; and the similitude of the LORD shall he behold: wherefore then were ye not afraid to speak against my servant Moses? And the anger of the LORD was kindled against them; and he departed. And the cloud departed from off the tabernacle; and, behold, Miriam became leprous, white as snow: and Aaron looked upon Miriam, and, behold, she was leprous. And Aaron said unto Moses, Alas, my LORD, I beseech thee, lay not the sin upon us, wherein we have done foolishly, and wherein we have sinned. Let her not be as one dead, of whom the flesh is half consumed when he cometh out of his mother's womb. And Moses cried unto the LORD, saying, Heal her now, O God, I beseech thee.

Numbers 12:1–13

As a result of his marriage to an Ethiopian, (and because of their jealousy), Moses' own brother and sister leveled unjust and slanderous attacks against his character. In essence, they were questioning his fitness to fulfill the role of spiritual authority over the children of Israel. Because Moses was unwilling to defend himself, God came to his defense. Miriam became leprous. Although he had been hesitant to speak up in his own defense, Moses agreed to intercede with God for Miriam and Aaron, though their offense was as much against him as against the Lord.

It was significantly interjected in verse 3 of this passage that Moses was the meekest man of his day. The fact that he did not speak until verse 13—and then only on behalf of his accusers—is a characteristic sign of his meek nature. It was this meekness that enabled him to remain silent while the Lord rebuked his persecutors and vindicated him before their very eyes.

If this incident were to take place today, how many believers would honestly be able to contain themselves from adding to the Lord's rebuke: "And, Lord, that's not all. You should have seen what they did to me yesterday; that would really have made you mad!"

Moses, however possessed so much meekness that he did not utter a single word—until his accusers had been punished by God. Then and only then did he speak up, crying out to God, not to defend him against his persecutors, but rather to plead on their behalf.

Meekness gave Moses strength to not retaliate when falsely accused. It gave him the self-control to refrain from self-defense and to allow the Lord to vindicate him. It is God's desire that believers today not return evil for evil, but rather to turn occasions for offense into opportunities for intercession. This loving transformation can only be accomplished through a meek and controlled heart.

In the book of Deuteronomy, we read these words from Moses himself as addressed to the children of Israel:

So I turned and came down from the mount, and the mount burned with fire: and the two tables of the covenant were in my two hands. And I looked, and, behold, ye had sinned against the LORD your God, and had made you a molten calf: ye had turned aside quickly out of the way which the LORD had commanded you. And I took the two tables, and cast them out of my two hands, and brake them before your eyes. And I fell down before the LORD, as at the first, forty days and forty nights: I did neither eat bread, nor drink water, because of all your sins which ye sinned, in doing wickedly in the sight of the LORD, to provoke him to anger. For I was afraid of the anger and hot displeasure, wherewith the LORD was wroth against you to destroy you. But the LORD hearkened unto me at that time also.

Deuteronomy 9:15–19

Moses had spent forty days and forty nights in the mountains fellowshipping with God through fasting and prayer on behalf of the people. He came down from the mountain carrying the Word, which God had revealed to him for the people, to discover that they were committing spiritual adultery with a molten calf. Moses was so angry that instead of delivering the message, he broke the tablets by throwing them violently to the ground. Meekness, however, caused him to regain his self-control, fall back down on his face before the Lord, and fast for forty more days and nights on behalf of the people.

By comparing this final response of Moses with the responses today of believers one to another in similar situations, one can easily detect meekness. Usually when believers today suffer even the slightest imposition, a rebuttal (usually under the pretense of righteous indignation or in the form of a "concerned" rebuke) is considered an acceptable response. God, however, wants to develop within His children such meek hearts that instead of responding with a rebuttal when they encounter unjust criticism, affliction, persecution, or ingratitude, they will possess the self-control to respond with intercession. The self-control to do this can be obtained only by developing the fruit of meekness.

> *And the servant of the Lord must not strive; but be gentle unto all men, apt to teach, patient, In meekness instructing those that oppose themselves; if God peradventure will give them repentance to the acknowledging of the truth; And that they may recover themselves out of the snare of the devil, who are taken captive by him at his will.*
>
> 2 *Timothy* 2:24–26

According to verse 26, it will only be through meekness that believers, especially those in the position of teachers, will have the strength to possess the self-control to continue teaching the Word to those who outwardly oppose the content of their message. The motive of their willingness to return time after time and teach the same message to the very people who continually oppose it is recorded in verses 25 and 26—that "God peradventure will give them repentance...And that they may recover themselves out of the snare of the devil." The spiritual welfare of the people is always the main concern of a teacher whose message is conceived in and delivered out of a spirit of meekness.

God wants every believer who shares the Word to do so with meekness, whether he is a teacher or preacher delivering a carefully prepared lesson or sermon to a congregation or layman witnessing one-on-one to his neighbor. Meekness is essential because every believer who shares the Word and lives a godly life will eventually encounter opposition and persecution: "Yea, and all that will live godly in Christ Jesus shall suffer persecution" (2 Timothy 3:12).

If the Word is shared with meekness, however, opposition will not prevent that Word from going forth. Those receiving persecution for the Word's sake will possess the self-control not to be offended at the opposition, but will return and minister repeatedly to those who oppose them. Furthermore, meekness will couple the delivery of the Word with intercession so that it will take even deeper root in the hearts of the hearers, and thereby be even more effective.

The main problem with believers who witness and minister the Word today is that they are so easily offended. It is vital for them to realize that they are "the salt of the earth" (Matthew 5:13) and "the light of the world" (Matthew 5:14). Without their witness, how will the earth be salted and the light shine that men might hope to see? Therefore, we believers have the awesome responsibility of overcoming being offended at opposition to the Word; to do this, we must develop the fruit of meekness.

The second function of meekness is enabling believers to be humble in spirit and lowly in mind. The noted scholar W. E. Vine defines *meekness* as "the opposite to self-assertiveness and self-interest;...it is not occupied with self at all." "Let nothing be done through strife or vainglory; but in lowliness of mind let each esteem other better than themselves. Look not every man on his own things, but every man also on the things of others" (Philippians 2:3, 4).

As the fruit of meekness is being developed in his life, a believer will come to develop the attitude that the welfare of others is more important than his own. Once this experience has taken place, the Christian will discover that a tremendous barrier has been broken down in his spiritual life.

For example, when he goes through a trial, such as sickness, rather than praying only for himself and his situation, he will find himself praying for someone else who is also going through a similar trial. Only meekness can equip a believer with the lowliness of mind necessary to put the welfare and happiness of others ahead of his own.

And it came to pass on the morrow, that Moses said unto the people, Ye have sinned a great sin: and now I will go up unto the LORD; peradventure I shall make an atonement for your sin. And Moses returned unto the LORD, and said, Oh, this people have sinned a great sin, and have made them gods of gold. Yet now,

if thou wilt forgive their sin——; and if not, blot me, I
pray thee, out of thy book which thou hast written.

Exodus 32:30–32

Moses esteemed others so much higher than himself that he was willing to offer his own salvation on their behalf. This is the ultimate manifestation of meekness: self-sacrifice. Salvation is an individual matter, of course, but there is a danger in the attitude, "I don't care what anyone else does; I'm going to make it." There is a truth in the sense of "even if no one else remains faithful, I purpose to go on with the Lord." Yet meekness will build within the believer an unselfish attitude that has the capability of reaching the point that the eternal salvation of others becomes more important to him than his own well-being.

We believers still have a struggle, however, with the idea of laying down our lives for the brethren by praying and fasting for one another. The Body of Christ is in great need of cultivating and developing the fruit of meekness. Many believers have allowed this fruit to wither on the vine simply by their passiveness in the midst of this self-centered age in which we live.

In chapter 20 of the book of Numbers, Moses was denied entrance into the Promised Land indirectly because of the rebelliousness of the people. Faced with the lack of water, the people complained to Moses about their thirst. God told Moses to speak to a certain rock and that water would come forth from it at his command. However, in his frustration with the people's constant complaints, Moses lost patience and instead of speaking to the rock, he struck it twice with his rod.

This action angered the Lord: "And the Lord spake unto Moses and Aaron,...therefore ye shall not bring this congregation into the land which I have given them" (Numbers 20:12). So Moses was denied the privilege of accompanying the children of Israel into the Promised Land.

Later on, in Chapter 21 of Numbers, when the people were bitterly complaining, the Lord sent fiery serpents among them. Many of the people died after being bitten by the serpents. The same people who caused Moses not to be able to enter the Promised Land now came to him and desperately pleaded with him to intercede for them with the Lord.

Entering the Promised Land was the one manifestation of the promises of God that Moses longed for in his lifetime. Now the very people who had caused him to sin, so that he could not see his lifelong desire fulfilled, stood before him asking for his help. The response of Moses to these people is recorded in verse 7: "...And Moses prayed for the people." Under such circumstances, this response could only have been made by a man of meekness.

The Apostle Paul exhorts us: "Brethren, if a man be overtaken in a fault, ye which are spiritual, restore such a one in the spirit of meekness; considering thyself, lest thou also be tempted" (Galatians 6:1). Every believer knows of at least one other person in the Body of Christ who has been "overtaken in a fault." In Galatians 6:1, Paul specifies the attitude and conduct God expects His children to display toward such people. We are to *restore* them in the spirit of meekness.

Vine tells us that the Greek word translated *restore* in this verse means "to mend, to furnish completely." He goes on to say of this word: "The tense is the continuous present, suggesting the necessity for patience and perseverance in the process."

Restoration usually will not occur in just one or two encounters. Most believers, however, are willing to continue ministering to someone only if they see some results after the first or second effort. Only a believer with meekness in his heart will continue ministering to someone even though a long period of time has elapsed and that person still shows no sign of responding.

The reason there are many breaches in the Body of Christ today is because believers are not willing to lay down their lives and allow a spirit of meekness to manifest itself in them; they are then unable to *keep* going and *keep* restoring one another. True meekness requires effort in the continuous present tense.

The third function of the fruit of meekness is to enable believers to be teachable: "Wherefore lay apart all filthiness and superfluity of naughtiness, and receive with meekness the engrafted word, which is able to save your souls" (James 1:21). Getting the word engrafted in the heart requires meekness. The "engrafted" Word is the thing that will result in the saving of the soul—that is, the ability to endure unto the end, to overcome, and not be overtaken. This ability is attainable only through a teachable spirit.

The greatest obstacle to a believer who is determined to develop a teachable spirit is the traditions of men. In Mark 7:9, 13 Jesus spoke to the scribes and Pharisees concerning this problem: "And he said unto them, Full well ye reject the commandment of God, that ye may keep your own tradition. Making the word of God of none effect through your tradition, which ye have delivered: and many such like things do ye."

Most Charismatics are guilty of automatically thinking of the denominational churches when they hear the word *tradition.* The dictionary definition of *tradition,* however, is "the handing down of statements, beliefs, legends, customs, etc. from generation to generation, especially by word of mouth."

Charismatic believers can be just as guilty of handing down statements and beliefs as denominational believers, making it possible for there to be Charismatic traditions. Most would agree that the Body of Christ is not yet perfect; so logically, there must be some false teachings in both the Charismatic Movement and the denominational churches. Often, these false teachings are passed down by word of mouth and become obstacles to developing a teachable spirit.

This truth is important for believers to grasp in light of the fact that Jesus Christ is coming back for a glorious church, not having spot, or wrinkle, or any such thing, but that it should be holy and without blemish (Ephesians 5:27). This "glorious church" is not a whitewashed building in which believers meet. Instead, the "glorious church" will be made up of people.

Jesus Christ is coming back for people who are holy, without blemish, without spot, and without any such thing. How are these people going to get this way? Ephesians 5:25, 26 reveals how we believers will achieve spotlessness in our lives: "Husbands, love your wives, even as Christ also loved the church, and gave himself for it; That he might sanctify and cleanse it with the washing of water by the word."

The teaching, preaching, admonishing, and exhorting of the Word of God is what will get the Church of Jesus Christ into proper doctrine, thereby washing us, cleansing us, and renewing our minds. "All scripture is given by inspiration of God, and is profitable for doctrine, for reproof, for correction, for instruction in righteousness: That the man of God may be perfect, thoroughly furnished unto all good works" (2 Timothy 3:16, 17).

Where do believers stand who have been taught something false, yet because they do not have a heart of meekness are not willing to change? Will their lack of a teachable spirit not leave them with spot and wrinkle? Believers who are not meek are in danger of becoming, "traditional," meaning that the Word of God will be of no effect in their lives. The grave danger of this situation lies in the fact that Jesus is returning for a spotless Bride; unfortunately, believers who are not meek and teachable might find themselves with spots when He returns.

Therefore, we believers must develop the fruit of meekness in our lives so that we will be teachable and capable of receiving the glorious truth of the Word of God.

> *And a certain Jew named Apollos, born at Alexandria, an eloquent man, and mighty in the scriptures, came to Ephesus. This man was instructed in the way of the Lord; and being fervent in the spirit, he spake and taught diligently the things of the Lord, knowing only the baptism of John. And he began to speak boldly in the synagogue: whom when Aquila and Priscilla had heard, they took him unto them, and expounded unto him the way of God more perfectly. And when he was disposed to pass into Achaia, the brethren wrote, exhorting the disciples to receive him: who, when he was come, helped them much which had believed through grace: For he mightily convinced the Jews, and that publicly, shewing by the scriptures that Jesus was Christ.*
>
> *Acts 18:24–28*

Apollos taught publicly in the synagogue with diligence and fervor. He had a good, scriptural revelation of repentance and thus taught the baptism of John. According to verse 25, however, this was the only New Testament truth he knew. He had a revelation. God did not want to take away from the truth he had; instead, He wanted to add to that truth.

Many believers today get a hold of a truth, and it becomes their "pet" doctrine. Then when God tries to give them His full counsel, they are not willing to receive anything new. Each believer has a special revelation of the Word in some particular area. Every one of us is like Apollos in that we each have a truth. But since no one in the Body of Christ is perfect yet, regardless of our degree of spiritual enlightenment or maturity, we all need to follow the example of Apollos. Although he was an eloquent man, learned in the scriptures, instructed in the way of the Lord, fervent in spirit, and a dynamic preacher and teacher, Apollos was still meek enough to allow Aquila and Priscilla to expound unto him the way of God more perfectly.

Unfortunately, many individual believers, churches, and Bible schools get hold of a truth, and because they do not possess meekness, harden their hearts against all other truth. They want to ride their pet doctrine until Jesus comes again. This is one of the reasons there are so many divisions in the church of Jesus Christ today. Every church in existence has at least a truth. Each is open to receive any teaching that conforms to the truth they have already discovered. Many times, however, the problem is that they are unwilling to receive, as truth, any teaching outside the boundaries of their established creeds, doctrines, and traditions.

Blessed is the believer, the church, the Bible school, and even the association or denomination that possess the meekness to remain teachable and thus open to receive the full truth of God. When all believers finally get their truths together, we will grow up and become a glorious Church. But this will never come to pass unless we Christians become teachable through the development of the fruit of meekness:

> *Howbeit when he, the Spirit of truth, is come, he will guide you into all truth: for he shall not speak of himself; but whatsoever he shall hear, that shall he speak: and he will shew you things to come. He shall glorify me: for he shall receive of mine, and shall shew it unto you. All things that the Father hath are mine: therefore said I, that he shall take of mine, and shall shew it unto you.*
>
> *John 16:13–15*

The Spirit of truth will guide believers into all truth if they are teachable enough for Him to do so. Jesus Christ is coming back for a glorious Church, one through which He is glorified. According to John 16:14, the Church glorifies Jesus by the Holy Spirit and takes His (truth) and shows it to the Church. The degree of truth that the Holy Spirit will reveal to the Church is recorded in John 16:15: "All things that the Father hath are mine: therefore said I, that he shall shew it unto you." The glorious Church will be a people to whom the Holy Spirit has revealed the full truth of God, to the glory of Jesus Christ the Son.

Therefore, a glorious Church, without spot, must be a Church that is obedient to the full counsel of God. If the enemy cannot get a local church off into some doctrinal error, then he will attempt to get them to place too much emphasis on one particular doctrine in order to keep them from receiving the full counsel of God, thereby preventing Jesus from being glorified.

God does not want to take away the truth that believers possess; He simply desires to add to that truth. Only those who are meek will allow Him to do so. Therefore, we believers need to develop the fruit of meekness in our lives so we will become teachable. Of course, this is not to say that we should become gullible. The Bible warns us against being blown about with every wind of doctrine (Ephesians 4:14). We must be like the Bereans, who searched out in the Scriptures every new teaching which they were presented (Acts 17:11).

As we believers become teachable, we will discover ourselves receiving revelation knowledge. With each new truth we receive and conform to, we will begin to become more complete in the whole counsel of God. The meek and the teachable are ever looking for the new counsel that God desires to reveal to His Church. Such seekers after truth will not be disappointed, for they may be assured that more revelation is on its way (Matthew 25:29).

Jesus was referring to Peter's revelation that He was the Son of God when He said: "...flesh and blood hath not revealed it unto thee, but my Father which is in heaven" (Matthew 16:17). Jesus then said in the following verse: "upon this rock I will build my church; and the gates of hell shall not prevail against it" (Matthew 16:18). Jesus Christ built His Church on the rock of revelation knowledge. That is also how He is going to complete His Church—by taking His truth and showing it to the Church. All this vast knowledge will only be revealed to the meek and received by the teachable.

Since meekness is a fruit and not a gift, it must be cultivated in order to become developed. Believers who are meek are that way because they have chosen to pay the cost required to cultivate the fruit of meekness in their individual lives. Meekness is certainly not some special anointing bestowed by God upon favored individuals. The Lord wants to work meekness within all of His children so that He can one day hand over to them the scepter of righteousness and make them rulers over many things (Matthew 25:21, 23).

In Matthew 5:5, Jesus said: "Blessed are the meek: for they shall inherit the earth." Our Lord is in the process of preparing the hearts of believers to whom He will hand over the rule and the dominion of this earth, but He can only give that power and authority to the meek. Those believers who refuse to cultivate and develop the fruit of meekness will never experience the full benefits of the overcoming life.

Fasting is one way for believers to cultivate the fruit of meekness in their individual lives. In Psalm 35:13, David said: "I humbled my soul with fasting" Since to be meek is to be humble in spirit, fasting is one means of cultivating meekness.

In the verse from Psalms, the Hebrew word translated *fasting* is *tsome*. In the New Testament, the Greek word for *fasting* is *nesteia* (*nace-ti-ah*), which Vine defines as "abstinence from food."

I believe it can be shown that any man, in either the Old or New Testament, who was reputed as being meek was a man who fasted; men of meekness are men of fasting

Food has been one of the enemy's most effective

tools in causing people to stumble and miss God's perfect plan. A few examples are the following: Adam and Eve (Genesis 3:6), the children of Israel (Exodus 16:3), and Esau (Hebrews 12:16). Satan discovered that food was such an effective means of temptation that he even tried to tempt Jesus with it (Matthew 4:3).

There is much truth to that old saying, "The way to a man's heart is through his stomach," for there is some kind of bond connecting the physical appetite with the desires of the heart. Since food is essential to life and health, any person who is willing to give up eating for someone else's sake is probably willing to lay down anything else within reason for that person. Believers who are willing to fast for other members of the Body of Christ would likely also be willing to give them the very shirts off their backs, with love. It is hardly conceivable for a believer to be willing to give up food for someone and then not be willing to display a meek attitude toward that individual when he meets with him in person.

> *Is not this the fast that I have chosen? to loose the bands of wickedness, to undo the heavy burdens, and to let the oppressed go free, and that ye break every yoke? And they that shall be of thee shall build the old waste places: thou shalt raise up the foundations of many generations; and thou shalt be called, The repairer of the breach, The restorer of paths to dwell in.*
>
> *Isaiah 58:6, 12*

Isaiah says that a believer who fasts will be called the "repairer of the breach" and "the restorer of paths to dwell in." Compare this verse with Galatians 6:1: "Brethren, if a man be overtaken in a fault, ye which are spiritual, restore such a one in the spirit of meekness; considering thyself, lest thou also be tempted." In light of these two scriptures, it seems obvious that restoration within the Body of Christ comes by meekness. One aspect of meekness is self-denial, which involves fasting or voluntary abstinence from food.

The second way for believers to cultivate the fruit of meekness is by benefiting from the wilderness experiences of life. The life of Moses is an example of how God will use wilderness experiences to develop meekness in His children.

According to Acts 7:22, Moses was very knowledgeable in the language and culture of Egypt, a symbolic representation of the world: "And Moses was learned in all the wisdom of the Egyptians, and was mighty in words and in deeds." He then spent forty years in the wilderness: "And when forty years were expired, there appeared to him in the wilderness of mount Sinai, an angel of the Lord in a flame of fire in a bush" (v. 30). Here, God revealed to Moses that he had been chosen to lead the children of Israel out of Egypt: "And Moses said unto the Lord, O my Lord, I am not eloquent, neither heretofore, nor since thou hast spoken unto thy servant: but I am slow of speech, and of a slow tongue" (Exodus 4:10).

After forty years in the wilderness, Moses was no longer self-sufficient, even though he "was learned in all the wisdom of the Egyptians." Wilderness experiences have a way of humbling people. Perhaps this is one reason God allows them to come into the lives of His children.

In reference to Jesus, Paul wrote: "Though he were a Son, yet learned the obedience by the things which he suffered" (Hebrews 5:8). In the Greek, the word translated *obedience* is *hupakoe* (*hoop-ak-o-ay*) meaning "*attentive, hearkening...compliance or submission.*" In other words, we can define obedience as "having a disposition to yield to others." Coming to a place of yielding oneself to other people is the very basis of meekness. Jesus Himself had to suffer in order to come to this place of obedience.

> *And thou shalt remember all the way which the LORD thy God led thee these forty years in the wilderness, to humble thee, and to prove thee, to know what was in thine heart, whether thou wouldest keep his commandments, or no. And he humbled thee, and suffered thee to hunger, and fed thee with manna, which thou knewest not, neither did thy fathers know; that he might make thee know that man doth not live by bread only, but by every word that proceedeth out of the mouth of the LORD doth man live.*
>
> *Deuteronomy 8:2, 3*

God allowed the children of Israel to go through the wilderness so they would become humble. He allowed His own Son to suffer in order to learn obedience. Humility and obedience are both forms of meekness. God allows believers today to go through the wilderness (a type or symbol of trials in various forms) for the same reason and purpose—so they will learn humility and obedience, thus developing meekness in their lives.

Believers should be aware, however, of the fact that just because they have experienced trials, does not necessarily mean that they have become humble or obedient. The children of Israel spent forty years in their wilderness, and yet when it was all over they were still rebellious. Unlike the Lord Jesus, they did not learn obedience by the things which they suffered; therefore, the fruit of meekness did not develop in them as God had intended.

Believers who allow meekness to mature in them during their wilderness experiences will have the attitude Paul had toward his trials:

> *But we have this treasure in earthen vessels, that the excellence of the power may be of God, and not of us. We are troubled on every side, yet not distressed; we are perplexed, but not in despair; Persecuted, but not forsaken; cast down, but not destroyed; Always bearing about in the body the dying of the Lord Jesus, that the life also of Jesus might be made manifest in our body.*
> *2 Corinthians 4:7–10*

In 2 Corinthians 12:7 Paul wrote: "And lest I should be exalted above measure through the abundance of the revelations, there was given to me a thorn in the flesh, the messenger of Satan to buffet me, lest I should be exalted above measure." Paul says that he was given a "thorn in the flesh" to keep him from becoming "exalted above measure." Yet he did not blame God for that "thorn," nor did he complain about it or attempt to avoid it. Instead, he learned humility through his afflictions and persecutions.

> *Blessed be God, even the Father of our Lord Jesus Christ, the Father of mercies, and the God of all comfort; Who comforteth us in all our tribulation, that we may be able to comfort them which are in any trouble, by the comfort wherewith we ourselves are comforted of God.*
>
> *2 Corinthians 1:3, 4*

Some receive greater benefit from their wilderness experiences than others. The reason is that some look to God for comfort in the midst of their trials and tribulations. As they allow God to comfort them, they learn what it means to be comforted. When believers allow God to comfort them, they are able to share that comfort with others who are going through similar trials. In other words, they learn to be meek toward others.

Many believers, however, do not turn to the God of comfort during their time of trial. Instead, they turn to the arm of flesh. Consequently, they do not experience the comfort of God. As a result, they have no comfort to give to others. Rather than offering aid and encouragement to those in need, such people are quick to criticize and judge when they see others falter and fail under pressure. Their basic problem is a lack of meekness.

On the other hand, when believers experience the comfort of the Lord in the midst of their trials, they become much less likely to judge others when they fail the same trial. They know that it was only by the grace and mercy of God that they were able to endure to the end.

Many times those who criticize and condemn others for their failures are those who have never been in the same situation. Never having experienced the comfort of the Lord themselves, they have no comfort to offer others.

Israel never trusted God in the wilderness and never fully experienced His comfort. For this reason, the fruit of meekness was not developed in them; thus their thoughts remained selfish throughout the entirety of the journey.

The third way for believers to develop the fruit of meekness is through denial of self. Meekness is the opposite of self-interest. According to Vine's definition of meekness, a meek individual is not concerned with self at all.

Moses denied himself when he refused to be identified as a member of the ruling house of Egypt: "Moses, when he was come to years, refused to be called the son of Pharaoh's daughter" (Hebrews 11:24).

There is an allurement of living for self that is especially powerful in this present age of self-indulgence. Today we believers have the same choice to make as Moses. We must decide whether "to be called the son of Pharaoh's daughter" (that is, to identify ourselves with the god of this world in order to enjoy the pleasures he offers), or to take our stand as children of light and do the will of our heavenly Father.

The will of God for Moses, at that time in his life, was that he spend forty years as a fugitive in the wilderness. Only by denying self, could Moses have made the decision which was to transform him into the meekest man of his day. Self-denial must *always* precede meekness.

This was also true in the life of Jesus, as we see in the writings of Paul to the church of Philippi:

> *Let this mind be in you, which was also in Christ Jesus: Who, being in the form of God, thought it not robbery to be equal with God: But made himself of no reputation, and took upon him the form of a servant, and was made in the likeness of men: And being found in fashion as a man, he humbled himself, and became obedient unto death, even the death of the cross.*
>
> *Philippians 2:5–8*

When He became a man, Jesus emptied Himself completely. Like Moses, He emptied Himself of the benefits, rights, and privileges that go with being the Son of the ruling Monarch. Rather than insisting on His rights, He denied Himself and chose the will of God. He made Himself of no reputation when He left His position in the kingdom of His Father. He chose to do the will of God, even though that meant spending thirty-three years in the wilderness of this earth and suffering an unjust death on the cross.

Like Moses and Jesus, we believers today must decide between living for self or living to do the will of

God. If we will but choose to enter the wilderness and allow ourselves to experience the comfort of the Lord there, we will emerge from the darkness possessing the fruit of meekness. Thus, we will be made fit vessels for the Master's use (2 Timothy 2:20, 21).

One characteristic of the life of Jesus, which is of great significance for us believers today, is the degree to which He denied Himself. Jesus submitted unconditionally to the Spirit of His Father within:

> *Then said Jesus unto them, When ye have lifted up the Son of man, then shall ye know that I am he, and that I do nothing of myself; but as my Father hath taught me, I speak these things. And he that sent me is with me: the Father hath not left me alone; for I do always those things that please him.*
>
> *John 8:28, 29*

Jesus glorified God when He declared that He did nothing of Himself, that He always did those things which please the Father.

The result of His unconditional submission was that the Spirit of God was given to Him without measure: "For he whom God hath sent speaketh the words of God: for God giveth not the Spirit by measure unto him" (John 3:34). Jesus possessed the Spirit in His fullness. Likewise, the extent to which we believers yield to the Spirit will be the extent to which we will experience His fullness and His fruits.

Many believers spend much time and effort wondering just how they are to yield and what exactly they are to do in order to offer themselves in total surrender to Christ. What must one do to yield himself totally to the Spirit? The answer is: "Nothing, absolutely nothing!" Yielding is not something one does. Yielding is not an action of the body, it is an attitude of the heart.

Yielding is the absence of resistance. It is not something we believers must strive to do, any more than we must strive to sleep or to breathe. Actually, anyone who has ever tried to fall asleep at night knows that trying to fall asleep makes it that much harder to attain. The same is true of yielding oneself to the Spirit. A believer has yielded himself as soon as he has ceased to resist.

Yielding is the absence of an expression of self-will. We should never pray, "Thy will be done in earth, as it is in heaven" (Matthew 6:10) unless we are fully willing to let God's will be done through us. We should, however, desire to pray this prayer, for it is needful in order for God's will to be done on earth. After all, we cannot expect God's will to be done through sinners. Therefore, we should earnestly desire to express the Father's will and not our own.

Yielding is an affection of the heart. So often, believers will try prayer, fellowship, and the study of the Word. After a trial period, however, many times they will abandon those efforts because there was no affection in their hearts for the things of God. They were merely "giving them a try," either out of a sense of obligation, guilt, or fear. The proper motive that will produce lasting, eternal results is a long affection for things above:

If ye then be risen with Christ, seek those things which are above, where Christ sitteth on the right hand of God. Set your affection on things above, not on things on the earth. For ye are dead, and your life is hid with Christ in God.

Colossians 3:1–3

Once we believers realize that we are dead to the things of the earth, then we will quickly yield to the things of the Spirit and set our affections on things above.

The Word of God contains the teachings, promises, prophecies, and counsel necessary for a happy and prosperous life on the earth. The full counsel of God, however, will only be received by those who have cultivated and developed the fruit of meekness in their individual lives. The propagation of the full counsel of God is dependent upon the meek. God's whole Word will be spread across this earth by those who have developed the fruit of meekness. Therefore, it is not surprising that Jesus said that it will be the meek who will inherit the earth (Matthew 5:5), for it will be through the meek that "the earth shall be full of the knowledge of the Lord, as the waters cover the sea" (Isaiah 11:9).

THE CALL FOR
SELF-CONTROL

"But the fruit of the Spirit is...temperance; against such there is no law."

Galatians 5:22, 23

The English word *temperance* in Galatians 5:23 is a translation of the Greek word *egkrateia* (*eng-krat'-i-ah*), meaning *"self-control"* or *"continence."* This word *egkrateia* is derived from *kratos,* "strength," which is the Greek word translated *power* in the second half of Ephesians 1:19:

And what is the exceeding greatness of his power to us-ward who believe, according to the working of his mighty power, Which he wrought in Christ, when he raised him from the dead, and set him at his own right hand in the heavenly places.

Ephesians 1:19, 20

The same strength and power that raised Jesus from the dead and exalted Him in heaven is available to us believers today as a fruit of the Spirit which we may cultivate in our individual lives. The fruit of self-control will enable us to crucify the flesh and fulfill Galatians 5:24: "And they that are Christ's have crucified the flesh with the affections and lusts."

God would not demand of His children that which would be impossible for them to fulfill. He never intended for believers to overcome the flesh by their flesh. Rather, God has provided His children with a supernatural seed of strength and self-control. That seed only requires cultivation in order for it to produce over-coming power by the Spirit. This power will surpass all previous, unsuccessful attempts at self-improvement. It will overcome any area of lust in the individual lives of those Christians who possess and apply it.

> *Know ye not that they which run in a race run all, but one receiveth the prize? So run, that ye may obtain. And every man that striveth for the mastery is temperate in all things. Now they do it to obtain a corruptible crown; but we an incorruptible. I therefore so run, not as uncertainly; so fight I, not as one that beateth the air: But I keep under my body, and bring it into subjection: lest that by any means, when I have preached to others, I myself should be a castaway.*
> *1 Corinthians 9:24–27*

The believer who is striving for mastery—that is, who is striving to be what God expects of him—must be temperate in all things. This involves bringing the physical body into subjection. *Subjection* in verse 27 is a transla-tion of the Greek word *doulagugei* (*doo'-lag-ogue-eh'-o*), which Strong tells us comes from a combination of two

Greek words meaning "*to be a slave-driver,* i.e. to *enslave* (fig. *subdue*):-bring into subjection."

In order to live up to the expectations of God, a believer must have so much control over his body that it becomes his slave. Since a slave has no legal rights and is bound by law to obey his master, a body brought into subjection must be obedient to its owner. When the Spirit of God dominates a person, He demands of that person self-control. As a result, he will crucify the affections and lust of his flesh that war against the Spirit.

According to Paul, the result of not bringing the body into subjection is to become a "castaway." The Greek word translated *castaway* in 1 Corinthians 9:27 is *adokimos* (*ad-ok'ee-mos*), which Strong defines as: *unapproved,* i.e. *rejected;...worthless...reprobate.*" Because of a lack of self-control, many believers have become worthless "castaways"; they have dropped out of the race for the incorruptible crown.

Moreover, brethren, I would not that ye should be ignorant, how that all our fathers were under the cloud, and all passed through the sea; And were all baptized unto Moses in the cloud and in the sea; And did all eat the same spiritual meat; And did all drink the same spiritual drink: for they drank of that spiritual Rock that followed them: and that Rock was Christ. But with many of them God was not well pleased: for they were overthrown in the wilderness. Now these things were our examples, to the intent we should not lust after evil things, as they also lusted. Neither be ye idolaters, as were some of them; as it is written, The people sat down to eat and drink, and rose up to play. Neither let us commit fornication, as some of them committed, and fell in one day three and twenty thousand. Neither let us tempt Christ, as some of them also tempted, and were destroyed of serpents. Neither murmur ye, as some of them also murmured, and were destroyed of the destroyer. Now all these things happened unto them for examples: and they are written for our admonition, upon whom the ends of the world are come. Wherefore let him that thinketh he standeth take heed lest he fall.

1 Corinthians 10:1–12

These things happened to Israel that they might be an example for believers today. Thus, we Christians need to examine carefully this portion of scripture to discover why the children of Israel were overcome in the wilderness. Generally speaking, they were overcome by the lust of the flesh, with its affections and desires (v. 6).

Although they experienced such mighty manifestations from God as the parting of the Red Sea, although they took part in the eating of the spiritual meat and drinking from the spiritual Rock, which was Christ, they had no self-control. Therefore, they displeased God because they allowed themselves to be overcome with their own lusts during their trials in the wilderness.

There hath no temptation taken you but such as is common to man: but God is faithful, who will not suffer you to be tempted above that ye are able; but will with the temptation also make a way to escape, that ye may be able to bear it.

1 *Corinthians* 10:13

In this verse we see that all of mortal creation experiences temptation. Since no one will ever mature to the place where he is no longer tempted, sin does not lie in the temptation itself but in yielding to that temptation. So, even though the children of Israel experienced such miraculous, supernatural intervention in their lives, they displeased God, not because they were tempted but because they allowed themselves to fall prey to their fleshly desires.

No one is exempt from temptation. Therefore, God would say to us today: "Wherefore let him that thinketh he standeth take heed lest he fall" (v. 12). God desires for His children to develop the fruit of temperance within their spirits so that they will have the strength to exercise self-control and thus overcome the flesh: "For if ye livesafter the flesh, ye shall die: but if ye through the Spirit do mortify the deeds of the body, ye shall live" (Romans 8:13).

Specifically, the children of Israel were overcome in four areas of the lust of the flesh. According to 1 Corinthians 10:7, they were overcome by idolatry, fornication, tempting Christ, and murmuring. In verse 6 of that passage Paul tells us: "Now these things were our examples, to the intent we should not lust after evil things, as they also lusted." God knows that His children are in danger today of being overcome of the same things by which the children of Israel were overcome. Therefore, these things are worthy of our careful consideration.

The first function of the fruit of temperance is to aid believers in overcoming idolatry. New Testament believers are reminded of the children of Israel and are admonished in verse 7: "Neither be ye idolaters, as were some of them; as it is written, The people sat down to eat and drink, and rose up to play." We find the commandment against idolatry in Exodus 20:4, 5:

> *Thou shalt not make unto thee any graven image, or any likeness of any thing that is in heaven above, or that is in the earth beneath, or that is in the water under the earth. Thou shalt not bow down thyself to them, nor serve them: for I the LORD thy God am a jealous God, visiting the iniquity of the fathers upon the children unto the third and fourth generation of them that hate me.*

In the Old Testament, God commanded His people not to bow down and serve idols. The Hebrew word translated *serve* is *abad* (*aw-bad'*) and means "*to work* (in any sense); *enslave;* keep in bondage" It is true that not too many believers today are tempted with idolatry in the sense of bowing their knee before an idol. However, since covetousness is the same as idolatry (Colossian 3:5), many Christians are tempted with idolatry in the sense of serving whatever they have come to "idolize" in their lives. Whatever they "work" for, whatever "enslaves" them, whatever keeps them "in bondage," that is their "idol."

In the eyes of God, the man who serves an idol through covetousness is just as much an idolater as the one who bows his knee before a graven image: "For this ye know, that no whoremonger, nor unclean person, nor covetous man, who is an idolater, hath any inheritance in the kingdom of Christ and of God" (Ephesians 5:5). The most common ways in which believers are tempted to serve the "idols" in their lives are through their actions, thoughts, and feelings. The degree of idolatry in a Christian's life may be measured by the amount of time he devotes to the coveting and pursuit of things other than the knowledge of God.

One way in which a believer may know whether or not he is being tempted with covetousness is to evaluate how much of his time is spent working and worrying to achieve some goal, to attain some position, or to obtain some desired object. We believers should not covet and serve "idols"—even those things which we need. Instead, we should serve God and trust in Him to give us the desires of our hearts and to provide us those things He knows we truly need.

A believer may also judge whether or not he is being tempted with covetousness by evaluating how much time he spends indulging himself in the blessings God has already provided in his life. One without temperance can become covetous or immoderate, even with that which is God's provision. Jesus said: "Thou shalt worship the Lord thy God, and him only shalt thou serve" (Matthew 4:10). Worship and service can be measured as much by time as by effort or expense. If a believer is not careful to be "temperate in all things" (1 Corinthians 9:25), including the time and attention he devotes to his God-given blessings, he may end up serving the provision rather than the Provider.

Food is a provision of God with which some believers become covetous and intemperate. According to 1 Timothy 4:3, God created meats (food) to be received by His children with thanksgiving. In Matthew 6:11, however, Jesus prayed to the Father, *Give us this day our daily bread*, not "Give us this day our daily *bakery*"!

Sleep is also a provision of God which can be misused in a covetous or intemperate manner. According to Psalm 127:2, God gives His beloved sleep. In Proverbs 6:9, however, the self-indulgent beloved one is asked: "How long wilt thou sleep, O sluggard? When wilt thou arise out of thy sleep?"

Prosperity is another provision of God with which believers can become covetous and intemperate. According to Psalm 35:27, God takes pleasure in the prosperity of His servant. In Matthew 6:24, however, Jesus warns: "No man can serve two masters: for either he will hate the one, and love the other; or else he will hold to the one, and despise the other. Ye cannot serve God and mammon." A Christian cannot serve both God and money, or the things money can buy. This is true even if the money or the possessions have come into his life as a direct result of God's promise to prosper His faithful children.

The fruit of temperance enables believers to be moderate in their actions, thoughts, and feelings—even in regard to God's provisions. This principle is important since Jesus warned of a day when men would be so lacking in temperance that they would be caught unprepared:

> *And take heed to yourselves, lest at any time your hearts be overcharged with surfeiting, and drunkenness, and cares of this life, and so that day come upon you unawares. For as a snare shall it come on all them that dwell on the face of the whole earth.*
>
> *Luke 21:34, 35*

According to the dictionary, the verb *surfeit* means "to indulge to excess in anything." Believers whose hearts are "overcharged with surfeiting"—those who indulge in excess—will be overtaken just as the children of Israel were overtaken by their lusts in the wilderness and were left there to die. However, those believers who have cultivated and developed the fruit of temperance in their individual lives will not be over-indulgent; they will be soberly aware of the coming of "that day."

The second function of the fruit of temperance is to aid believers in overcoming fornication. In 1 Corinthians 10:8, the Apostle Paul reminds us of the fate of the children of Israel, warning: "Neither let us commit fornication, as some of them committed, and fell in one day three and twenty thousand."

In the eyes of God, friendship with the world is spiritual fornication: "Ye adulterers and adulteresses, know ye not that the friendship of the world is enmity with God? Whosoever therefore will be a friend of the world is the enemy of God" (James 4:4).

In reality, when a child of God lacks the self-control to resist adultery, he is in danger of becoming the friend of the world and thus the enemy of God.

Love not the world, neither the things that are in the world. If any man love the world, the love of the Father is not in him. For all that is in the world, the lust of the flesh, and the lust of the eyes, and the pride of life, is not of the Father, but is of the world. And the world passeth away, and the lust thereof: but he that doeth the will of God abideth for ever.

1 John 2:15–17

Beleivers who love the world and find themselves engaging in her lust of the flesh, her lust of the eyes, and her pride of life, are committing spiritual adultery against the Father.

Paul would remind us today just as he did those believers in his day: "For, brethren, ye have been called unto liberty; only use not liberty for an occasion to the flesh, but by love serve one another" (Galatians 5:13). Every believer has been set free, but not so he may do whatever *he* wants to do, but so he, by the Spirit, can do what *God* desires for him to do.

Be ye not unequally yoked together with unbelievers: for what fellowship hath righteousness with unrighteousness? and what communion hath light with darkness? And what concord hath Christ with

Belial? or what part hath he that believeth with an
infidel? And what agreement hath the temple of God
with idols? for ye are the temple of the living God;
as God hath said, I will dwell in them, and walk in
them; and I will be their God, and they shall be my
people. Wherefore come out from among them, and be
ye separate, saith the Lord, and touch not the unclean
thing; and I will receive you.

2 Corinthians 6:14–17

God desires for His children to be a holy people. It is by the grace of God that believers now have the strength to be holy, even as their Father in heaven is holy. In order to be received by this Holy One, we believers must separate ourselves from worldly pleasures and pursuits and dedicate ourselves to our Creator in faith and trust. By so doing, we will be using our freedom to choose what God desires for us, rather than what the world would tempt us with.

For the grace of God that bringeth salvation hath
appeared to all men, Teaching us that, denying
ungodliness and worldly lusts, we should live soberly,
righteously, and godly, in this present world.

Titus 2:11, 12

According to Titus, it is God's grace that teaches us that we should lead sober, righteous, godly lives. Believers who choose to deny ungodliness and worldly lusts will be using their freedom to choose what God desires for them. As they do so, they will be the recipients of His grace.

We believers are *in* the world, but we are not *of* the world. The fruit of temperance enables us to develop the necessary self-control to live in this world and yet not conformed to it.

The third function of the fruit of temperance is to aid in preventing believers from tempting Christ. Again Paul reminds us of the children of Israel, admonishing: "Neither let us tempt Christ, as some of them also tempted, and were destroyed of serpents" (1 Corinthians 10:9). The children of Israel tempted Christ by speaking against rightful authority.

> *And the people spake against God, and against Moses,*
> *Wherefore have ye brought us up out of Egypt to die*
> *in the wilderness? for there is no bread, neither is there*
> *any water; and our soul loatheth this light bread. And*
> *the* LORD *sent fiery serpents among the people, and*
> *they bit the people; and much people of Israel died.*
> *Numbers 21:5, 6*

The children of Israel spoke against the Lord and against Moses, their God-ordained leader. As a result, the Lord sent "fiery serpents" upon them.

> *Now the works of the flesh are manifest, which are these;*
> *Adultery, fornication, uncleanness, lasciviousness,*
> *Idolatry, witchcraft, hatred, variance, emulations,*
> *wrath, strife, seditions, heresies, Envyings, murders,*
> *drunkenness, revellings, and such like: of the which*

I tell you before, as I have also told you in time past, that they which do such things shall not inherit the kingdom of God.

Galatians 5:19–21

One of the works of the flesh is *sedition* (v. 20). *Sedition* is defined as "incitement of resistance to or insurrection against lawful authority." The fruit of temperance enables believers to submit to the God-ordained authority in their lives. The flesh may resist submission to rightful authority, but temperance will cause believers to mortify the deeds of the flesh and thus live in harmony with God's plan and purpose for their lives.

According to Paul, God has set parents in position of authority over their children, with the husband ordained as head of the family unit:

Wives, submit yourselves unto your own husbands, as unto the Lord. For the husband is the head of the wife, even as Christ is the head of the church: and he is the saviour of the body. Therefore as the church is subject unto Christ, so let the wives be to their own husbands in every thing. Children, obey your parents in the Lord: for this is right.

Ephesians 5:22–24; 6:1

The fruit of temperance will aid family members to conform to the scripturally prescribed order of authority. By so doing, they will be pleasing God rather than tempting Christ.

In Romans 13:1, 2 Paul tells us that governmental authorities are also ordained and established by God:

Let every soul be subject unto the higher powers. For there is no power but of God: the powers that be are ordained of God. Whosoever therefore resisteth the power, resisteth the ordinance of God: and they that resist shall receive to themselves damnation.

The Apostle Peter writes to believers:

Submit yourselves to every ordinance of man for the Lord's sake: whether it be to the king, as supreme; Or unto governors, as unto them that are sent by him for the punishment of evildoers, and for the praise of them that do well. Honour all men. Love the brotherhood. Fear God. Honour the king.

1 *Peter* 2:13, 14, 17

The fruit of temperance will aid believers in submitting to governmental authorities. Those who do so will not only be benefiting their lives by coming under the protection of these duly-instituted powers, they will guard themselves against becoming guilty of resisting God and tempting Christ.

The fourth function of the fruit of temperance is to aid believers in resisting the temptation to murmur. Once more, we are reminded by Paul of the children of Israel and are admonished: "Neither murmur ye, as some of them also murmured, and were destroyed of the destroyer" (1 Corinthians 10:10). To *murmur* simply means "*to grumble.*" The implication is that the children of Israel were guilty of complaining about their lot and their leaders. Both types of negative speech are condemned as being detrimental to the individual believer, as well as the whole Church.

Surely, the children of Israel felt that they had good reason to murmur in the wilderness; they must have felt justified as they grumbled and complained about their situation. Certainly, no local body of believers today finds itself in circumstances offering a greater opportunity or temptation to murmur than those in which the children of Israel found themselves.

However, it must be noted that nowhere in the Scriptures is it stated that unpleasant circumstances are an excuse for murmuring. On the contrary, such periods of adversity are the very time believers are expected to hold their tongues, even as they hold their ground.

According to James 3:6, the tongue is the one member of the body that is capable of defiling the whole body: "And the tongue is a fire, a world of iniquity: so is the tongue among our member, that it defileth the whole body, and setteth on fire the course of nature: and it is set on fire of hell." This, of course, is referring to the effect of negative speech on the individual believer.

The tongue is also capable of corrupting the whole Body of Christ: "But if ye bite and devour one another, take heed that ye be not consumed one of another" (Galatians 5:15). This verse implies that the tongue is the worst enemy of the Church. One reason it is so deadly is because it destroys from within. When believers grumble and complain about their leaders or about each other, regardless of how justifiable their complaint might be, they are actually consuming, or destroying, one another. As a result, the whole Body suffers.

According to James, the flesh of man is not strong enough to put a stop to this destructive work of the tongue within the Body of Christ: "But the tongue can no man tame; it is an unruly evil, full of deadly poison" (James 3:8). The power necessary to control this potential source of corruption among believers must come from the Spirit of God as individual believers cultivate and develop the fruit of temperance.

The first way in which individual believers may develop the fruit of temperance in their lives is by learning to control their mouths:

> For in many things we offend all. If any man offend not in word, the same is a perfect man, and able also to bridle the whole body. Behold, we put bits in the horses' mouths, that they may obey us; and we turn about their whole body. Behold also the ships, which though they be so great, and are driven of fierce winds, yet are they turned about with a very small helm, whithersoever the governor listeth.
>
> James 3:2–4

According to verse 2, the tongue has the capability of "bridling" the whole body. The word translated "bridle" in this passage refers to a "*curb*" or a "*bit*." In this context, James compares the potential power of the tongue of man to that of a bridle or bit by which a rider can direct a horse that is far heavier and stronger than he is. James also gives the analogy of a huge ship whose course is determined by a small helm or rudder, even though the winds may be fiercely blowing against it from the opposite direction.

These analogies are tremendous, for they illustrate a vital principle of human nature and of the Christian faith. In these word pictures, we see that whatever our individual strengths or weaknesses, we can bring about a change in any area of our personal lives, simply by controlling our tongues.

"Whoso keepeth his mouth and his tongue keepeth his soul from troubles" (Proverbs 21:23). Many believers today are experiencing trouble in their spiritual lives because of their mouths. They constantly confess such things as: "I can't study." "I can't intercede well." "I can't break this bad habit in my life." "I can't stop murmuring; I've been doing it for too long now." According to Proverbs 21:23, confessions such as these are troublesome for the soul.

"Thou art snared with the words of thy mouth, thou art taken with the words of thy mouth" (Proverbs 6:2). Many other believers are experiencing trouble in their physical bodies because of their mouths. For example, people who constantly confess that they are tired, often find themselves "snared" and "taken" by their words.

The confessing of the mouth is so powerful that it can even change the condition of the heart: "For with the heart a man believeth unto righteousness; and with the mouth confession is made unto salvation" (Romans

10:10). An individual's salvation involves the confession of his mouth, but salvation involves much more than just redemption from sin; it includes deliverance from every curse of the law.

"A man hath joy by the answer of his mouth: and a word spoken in due season, how good is it!" (Proverbs 15:23). The amount of joy in a believer's heart may be affected by the confession of his mouth. Many Christians could change the condition of their hearts from heaviness to joy simply by confessing the positive aspects of their lives instead of the negative.

The connection between the tongue of man and the spirit of man is inseparable, for Jesus said: "out of the abundance of the heart the mouth speaketh" (Matthew 12:34). Therefore, the believer who keeps his tongue is actually keeping his heart. According to Proverbs 4:23, this will affect his entire life: "Keep thy heart with all diligence; for out of it are the issues of life."

The second way in which believers may develop the fruit of temperance in their lives is by strengthening their inner man:

> *This I say then, Walk in the Spirit, and ye shall not fulfill the lust of the flesh. For the flesh lusteth against the Spirit, and the Spirit against the flesh: and these are contrary the one to the other: so that ye cannot do the things that ye would.*
>
> *Galatians 5:16, 17*

A believer is comprised of both flesh and spirit.

Whichever one of these two he "feeds" the most will be the one that will dominate and eventually become most manifest in his life.

According to Galatians 5:17, flesh and spirit are "contrary" to one another. Contrary means "tending to an opposing course." As Paul tells us in verse 16, the desires of the flesh and the desires of the reborn spirit are in direct opposition to each other.

In Romans 7:14–25 Paul describes the battle that went on inside him as his body and his regenerated spirit raged against each other:

> *For I delight in the law of God after the inward man:*
> *But I see another law in my members, warring against*
> *the law of my mind, and bringing me into captivity to*
> *the law of sin which is in my members.*
>
> *vv. 22, 23*

In verse 24 of that passage, he asks: "O wretched man that I am! who shall deliver me from the body of this death?" The answer was given in the next verse: "I thank God through Jesus Christ our Lord."

Like Paul, as a believer yields to the Spirit of God within he will develop the strength he needs to exercise control over his flesh and to bring it into submission to his reborn spirit. As this strength and control increase in his life, so will the fruit of temperance.

Paul knew the source of the fruit of temperance. That's why he prayed for the believers in Ephesus: "That he (God) would grant you, according to the riches of his glory, to be strengthened with might by his Spirit in the inner man" (Ephesians 3:16). Paul admonished believers to strengthen their inner man by the Spirit of God because he knew that it is only when the inner man is strong that the flesh will be brought under control.

The first way a believer may be strengthened with might by the Spirit in the inner man is through assimilation of the Word of God:

> *And beside this, giving all diligence, add to your faith virtue; and to virtue knowledge; And to knowledge temperance; and to temperance patience; and to patience godliness.*
>
> *2 Peter 1:5, 6*

As we see in this passage, knowledge precedes temperance. Knowledge comes from diligent study of the Word of God.

The second way in which a believer may be strengthened with might by the Spirit in the inner man is through speaking in tongues: "He that speaketh in an unknown tongue edifieth himself; but he that prophesieth edifieth the church" (1 Corinthians 14:4). To edify means "to build up." Speaking in tongues strengthens the inner man by building him up to such a degree that the Spirit dominates the flesh. The believer, in whom the Spirit dominates, will discover that temperance is manifested in his life in direct proportion to the degree that his inner man is edified.

The third way in which a believer may be strengthened with might by the Spirit in the inner man is through praise. The Psalmist David said of the Lord: "Out of the mouths of babes and sucklings hast thou ordained strength because of thine enemies, that thou mightest still the enemy and the avenger" (Psalm 8:2). The Hebrew word translated strength in this verse means "boldness,...might, power." This strength within the individual believer is powerful enough to still any enemy—even if that enemy happens to be the believer's own flesh.

In Matthew 21:16, Jesus revealed the source of this strength when he quoted this verse from Psalms, with one important change: "Yea; have ye never read, Out of the mouth of babes and sucklings thou hast perfected praise?" Notice that our lord altered this verse by noting that the way God ordains strength is by perfecting praise.

The third way in which believers may develop the fruit of temperance is through receiving God's grace:

Therefore being justified by faith, we have peace with God through our Lord Jesus Christ: By whom also we have access by faith into this grace wherein we stand, and rejoice in hope of the glory of God.

Romans 5:1, 2

Most Christians do not know any more of grace than that expressed by Paul in Ephesians 2:8 which reads: "For by grace are ye saved through faith; and that not of yourselves: it is the gift of God." According to Romans 5:2, all believers have been given "access" into grace to stand. The Greek word translated *access* here means "*admission*"; the root word from which it is taken is a verb meaning "to *approach:* -bring, draw near."

According to Hebrews 4:16, grace is available for believers to provide them access to the Father so they can approach Him in their darkest hour: Let us therefore come boldly unto the throne of grace, that we may obtain mercy, and find grace to help in time of need.

Grace has been defined as "God's ability to do His will." Every believer has experienced a time in his life when he did not have the self-control to do God's will. Each of us can, however, find "grace to help in time of need." We need only to learn to experience the fullness of that grace in which we already abide. The more we believers experience the grace of God, the more the fruit of temperance will be developed in our lives.

There is no greater frustration for a believer than having a good and honest heart that desires to do those things that are pleasing in the Father's sight, but not possessing the strength or the self-control necessary to keep His commandments. Such a believer will find great peace and relief for his heart if he will take courage and begin to cultivate and develop the fruit of temperance in his life.

The fruit of temperance is a public exhibition of the mercy in the heart of God for His children; it is His gift especially to those who have been burdened by guilt and frustration because they have not been able to do their Father's will. The answer to self-condemnation is to begin to cultivate the fruit of temperance. As this is done, God will replace that condemnation with strength and self-control by the power of His Holy Spirit.

ENDNOTES

[1] James Strong, "Greek Dictionary of the New Testament," Strong's Exhaustive Concordance of the Bible (Nashville: Abingdon, 1890): 73.

[2] The Companion Bible (Grand Rapids, Michigan: Zondervan bible Publishers, 1974). Appendixes 108, iii, p. 153.

[3] Strong, p. 71

[4] The Companion Bible, Appendixes 108, I, p. 153.

[5] The Companion Bible, (Grand Rapids: Zondervan Bible Publishers, 1974), Appendixes 132, I, ii, p. 163.

[6] Strong, p. 19.

[7] Strong, p. 7.

[8] The Companion Bible, Appendixes 135, II, P. 164.

[9] Strong, p. 75.

[10] The Companion Bible, Appendixes 135, 12, p. 164.

[11] James Strong, Strong's Exhaustive Concordance of the Bible (Nashville: Abingdon, 1890), "Greek Dictionary of the New Testaments," p. 74.

[12] James Strong, Strong's Exhaustive Concordance (Nashville: Abingdon, 1890), "Hebrew and Chaldee Dictionary," p. 57.

[13] Strong, "Greek Dictionary of the New Testament," p. 43.

[14] James Strong, Strong's Exhaustive Concordance of the Bible (Nashville: Abingdon, 1890), "Greek Dictionary of the New Testament," p. 79.

[15] Strong, p. 76.

[16] *W. E. Vine, Expository Dictionary of New Testament Words (Old Tappan: Revell, 1940): 307.*

[17] *Strong, p. 73.*

[18] *Strong, p. 26.*

[19] *Webster's Seventh New Collegiate Dictionary (Springfield: G. & C. Merriam Company, 1969): 620.*

[20] *Kenneth Wuest's Word Studies in the Greek New Testament, Vol. I (Grand Rapids: Eerdmans Publishing Company):160.*

[21] *Webster's Seventh New Collegiate Dictionary (Springfield: G. & C. Merriam Company, 1969): 274.*

[22] *Strong, p. 66.*

[23] *Strong, "Hebrew and Chaldee Dictionary," p. 118; "Greek Dictionary of the New Testament," p. 41.*

[24] *Strong, p. 41.*

[25] *W.E. Vine, Vine's Expository Dictionary of New Testament Words (Old Tappan: Revell, 1940): 165.*

[26] *James Strong, Strong's Exhaustive Concordance (Nashville: Abingdon, 1890), "Greek Dictionary of the New Testament," p. 78.*

[27] *Strong, p. 11.*

[28] *Vine, p. 183.*

[29] *Strong, "Greek Dictionary of the New Testament," p. 21.*

[30] *Strong, p. 21.*

[3] *W.E. Vine, Vine's Expository Dictionary of New Testament Words (Old Tappan: Revell, 1940): 71.*

[32] *James Strong, Strong's Exhaustive Concordance of the Bible (Nashville: Abingdon, 1890), "Hebrew and Chaldee Dictionary," p. 53.*

[33] *Webster's New Twentieth Century Dictionary, 2nd Ed., s.v. "charisma."*

[34] *Strong, "Hebrew and Chaldee Dictionary," p. 72.*

[35] *Strong, "Greek Dictionary of the New Testament," p. 58.*

[36] *Strong, "Hebrew and Chaldee Dictionary," p. 14.*

[37] *Strong, "Greek Dictionary of the New Testament," p. 27.*

[38] *James Strong, Strong's Exhaustive Concordance of the Bible, "Greek Dictioanry of the New Testament," p. 60.*

[39] *Hogg and Vine, Notes on Galatians, pp. 294, 295 as quoted by W. E. Vine, Expository Dictionary of New Testament Words (Old Tappan: Revell, 1940): 56*

[40] *Vine, p. 290.*

[4] *The American College Dictionary, s.v. "tradition".*

[42] *Strong, "Hebrew and Chaldee Dictionary," p. 98.*

[43] *Strong, "Greek Dictionary of the New Testament," p. 50.*

[44] *Vine, p. 80.*

[45] *Strong, p. 73.*

[46] *James, Strong, Strong's Exhaustive Concordance of the Bible (Nashville: Abingdon, 1890), "Greek Dictionary of the New Testament," p. 25.*

[47] *W.E. Vine, Expository Dictionary of New Testament Words (Old Tappan: Revell, 1940): 114.*

[48] *Strong, p. 24.*

[49] *Strong, p. 8.*

[50] *Strong, "Hebrew and Chaldee Dictionary," p. 84.*

[51] *The American College Dictionary, s. v. "surfeit."*

[52] *Webster's New College Dictionary, s. v. "sedition."*

[53] *Strong, "Greek Dictionary of the New Testament," p. 20.*

[54] *Strong, p. 77.*

[55] *Webster's New Collegiate Dictionary, s. v. "contrary."*

[56] *The American College Dictionary, s. v. "edify."*

[57] *Strong, "Hebrew and Chaldee Dictionary," p. 86.*

[58] *Strong, "Greek Dictionary of the New Testament," p. 61.*

To obtain a full list of Greg's tapes and books or to have him minister at your church write to:

Greg Zoschak
PO Box 33
Hinton, OK 73047
Phone: 405–884–2862
E-Mail: zzoelife@hotmail.com